More Weekends for Two
in Northern California

50 All-New Romantic Getaways

More Weekends for Two in Northern California

50 All-New Romantic Getaways

BY BILL GLEESON

PHOTOGRAPHS BY JOHN SWAIN

CHRONICLE BOOKS

SAN FRANCISCO

Contents

ACKNOWLEDGMENTS

Regina Miesch, photographic stylist
Krista Hendricks, editorial/research assistance
Yvonne Gleeson, research assistance
Michael and Nancy Finn
John and Debbie Lewis
Robert and Ferne Gleeson
Richard and Isabel Gomes
Kari and Jeff Gleeson

Library of Congress Cataloging-in-Publication Data
available.

Printed in Hong Kong.

ISBN 0-8118-0511-5

Book and cover design: Robin Weiss
Cover Photo: Agate Cove Bed-and-Breakfast Inn

Distributed in Canada by Raincoast Books,
8680 Cambie Street
Vancouver, B.C. V6P 6M9

10 9 8 7 6 5 4 3 2 1

Chronicle Books
275 Fifth Street
San Francisco, CA 94103

Introduction

*I*f you've ever agonized over the menu of flavors in an ice cream parlor, you'll have some appreciation of the bittersweet decisions that faced us in creating the original edition of *Weekends for Two in Northern California.* In a region that holds some of the world's most coveted romantic destinations, narrowing a listing to only fifty was an overwhelming, albeit enjoyable task. Although pleased with the results, we regretted the many other sensuous secrets that because of space limitations couldn't be shared.

Fortunately, that first volume struck a chord among traveling romantics and spawned a still-expanding series of Weekends for Two guides. In between searching out romantic destinations in other parts of the country we were invited to produce a Northern California sequel.

This volume, designed to expand your romantic horizons, spotlights fifty more seductive inns and hotels. In assembling this listing, we were guided by our original goal: to take the guesswork out of planning a special getaway and to help ensure that your experience is a memorable one—for all the right reasons.

Rooms for Romance

When evaluating a property, we look for a certain ambience as well as specific features that engender romance. Our checklist includes:
- Private bathrooms (we name any rooms that share)
- In-room fireplaces
- Tubs or showers big enough for two
- Breakfast in bed or in your room
- Feather beds and cushy comforters
- Canopied, four-poster, king-sized beds
- Couches, love seats, or nooks for sitting together
- Private decks, patios, or balconies with inspirational views
- Romantic decor, special touches, and thoughtful accessories

Few destinations offer this complete menu of niceties, but each must offer at least some of these features.

We also seek out hotels and inns that exude that overall, sometimes difficult-to-describe, intimate atmosphere and those that discourage child guests, since many dedicated moms and dads are seeking a well-deserved break from the kids.

Finally, we avoid destinations referred to in the lodging industry as *homestays.* These are houses in which a room or rooms are rented out to travelers, often by owners lacking skill in the art of innkeeping.

Within the inns and hotels listed in this book, we discovered special rooms that are particularly conducive to a romantic experience. Instead of leaving the choice of rooms to the reservation clerk and describing in detail the public areas of each establishment, we've devoted a good part of this book to details of specific rooms and suites. When booking your getaway reservation, don't hesitate to ask about the availability of a specific room—unless, of course, you already have a personal favorite.

Tables for Two

At the beginning of each regional listing, we've identified a few noteworthy restaurants near our featured destinations. These were sampled by us and/or recommended by innkeepers whose opinions we respect. Keep in mind, however, that restaurants—and chefs—come and go. Accordingly, we suggest you balance these recommendations with updates and new choices offered by your innkeepers. They're happy to offer suggestions.

Your Favorites

If we've overlooked one of your cherished romantic destinations in our two volumes of *Weekends for Two in Northern California*, please write to us in care of Chronicle Books, 275 Fifth Street, San Francisco, CA 94103. We look forward to sharing new romantic weekends for two in future printings.

A Word About Rates

Travelers scouting the highways for discount lodgings can still find a no-frills motel room for under $50. However, these guides aren't for bargain hunters. We view your romantic times together as the most special of occasions, and through years of travel we've confirmed the adage, you get what you pay for. Consequently, we've come to expect that a special room commands a higher price. In fact, you'll find few rooms described in these pages for less than $100 per night.

To help you plan your getaway budget, approximate 1995 rates for specific rooms are noted within each description. Keep in mind that an increasing number of establishments require two-night minimum stays on weekends and holidays.

Rates are classified at the end of each listing in the following ranges, not including tax:

Moderate: Under $150
Expensive: $150–$200
Deluxe: Over $200

Final Notes

No payment was sought or accepted from any establishment in exchange for a listing in this book.

Food, wine, and flowers were often added to our photo scenes for styling purposes. Some inns provide these amenities; others do not. Please ask when making a reservation whether these items are complimentary or whether they're provided for an extra charge.

Please understand we cannot guarantee that these properties will maintain furnishings or standards as they existed on our visit, and we very much appreciate hearing from readers if their experience is at variance with our descriptions. Reader comments are carefully consulted in the creation and revision of each Weekends for Two volume. Your opinions are appreciated.

The North Coast

DAYTIME DIVERSIONS

Salt Point State Park and Kruse Rhododendron Reserve near Timberhill Ranch offer six thousand acres of trails that extend to the ocean. Timberhill's own eighty acres offer hiking opportunities as well. Just north of Mendocino, in Russian Gulch State Park, a gentle six-and-a-half-mile hike will bring you to a romantic waterfall. At day's end, savor the sunset from Mendocino Headlands State Park on Little Lake Road.

Our favorite north coast galleries include Alinder (photography) and Woodbridge, both on Highway 1 in Gualala, and Henley's, just off Highway 1 on Annapolis Road at the Sea Ranch.

From its base in Fort Bragg, the Skunk Line conducts vintage rail excursions through towering redwoods.

TABLES FOR TWO

In Gualala, try St. Orres (see separate listing in this section) or the Old Milano Hotel, both located on Highway 1. From personal experience, we can also recommend the multicourse dinners served to guests and the general public high on a coastal ridge at Timberhill Ranch in Cazadero (see separate listing in this section).

In addition to offering sublime accommodations, the Albion River Inn (Highway 1 in Albion) operates a highly rated restaurant on a cliff overlooking the ocean.

Mendocino visitors in-the-know fill the dining room at Cafe Beaujolais (961 Ukiah Street). Call well in advance for reservations. The public dining room at the Hotel Carter in Eureka (see Carter House Cottage entry) is likewise a consistent winner.

For breakfast or lunch in Mendocino, sample the fare at the Mendocino Bakery and Cafe (Lansing Street near Ukiah Street). Popular north coast lunch spots along Highway 1 include the Food Company, a half-mile north of Gualala, and the Roadhouse Cafe in Elk.

TIMBERHILL RANCH

35755 Hauser Bridge Road
Cazadero, CA 95421
Telephone: (707) 847-3258

Fifteen cottages, each with private bath, deck, and
woodburning fireplace. No telephones or televisions
in cottages. Amenities include bathrobes, small
refrigerators, and cassette players. Operates on mod-
ified American plan (continental breakfast and dinner
included). Breakfast is delivered to your cottage.
Swimming pool, spa, and tennis courts. Smoking
permitted in certain cottages only. Handicapped
access. Two-night minimum stay on weekends;
three-night minimum stay during holiday periods.
Deluxe.

Getting There
From Highway 1, ninety miles north of San
Francisco and five miles north of Jenner, turn right
on Meyers Grade Road and follow for thirteen-and-
a-half miles to ranch. (Note: Meyers Grade Road
becomes Seaview Road, which later turns into
Hauser Bridge Road.)

Timberhill Ranch

Cazadero

Contrary to the images that its name might conjure, Timberhill Ranch isn't a rustic retreat for burly lumberjacks or a dusty cattle spread. This is one of the most sumptuous romantic hideaways we've discovered along the north coast.

This intimate resort, set high on a coastal ridge about one mile from the ocean, had its beginnings as a ranch and later as an alternative high school. Two Marin County career couples bought the property in the mid-1980s and built several freestanding guest cottages, creating a small country inn resort. My partner likened Timberhill to a luxurious summer camp for adults.

Rooms for Romance

Our home for a night, Cottage 14, was typical of Timberhill's accommodations. The large one-room cottage, with cedar log–style paneling, held a queen-sized bed, an armoire, two cushy chairs, and a table and chairs set. An expertly built fire awaited only a match. The spacious and contemporary separate bathroom was equipped with double sinks and a large shower with double seats.

Each Timberhill cottage is sited so as to provide optimal privacy. Our expansive side-facing deck offered wonderful views of nature, but no other cabins were visible. Cars aren't allowed within the compound, and cottages are reached via winding gravel pathways. Electric carts tote guest luggage between cottages and the parking area.

Cottages 8, 9, and 10, which face a large pond, are the most oft-requested. Cottages 9 and 10 receive the most sun. Cottages 3 and 5 also afford nice pond views.

A walking trail leads from the ranch to a small, romantic cliffside deck overlooking the ocean— perfect for a picnic lunch.

Dinners at Timberhill are served in a beautiful open dining room whose many windows afford panoramic mountain vistas. An adjacent building houses the reception and parlor areas. There's also a large swimming pool and a spa on-site.

Per-night rates at Timberhill, which include continental breakfast and six-course dinner for two, are in the mid $300 range (mid $200 range without meals). Midweek rates are less. There's also a charge of around $20 if you request a specific cottage.

North coast travelers should be advised that Timberhill Ranch isn't an ocean-view property, nor is it a destination that will appeal to folks expecting shopping and nightlife. However, for those who savor solitude, and romantic enchantment in an unspoiled natural setting, it doesn't get any better.

St. Orres

36601 South Highway 1
Gualala, CA 95445
Telephone: (707) 884-3303

Eleven cottage units with private bath; eight with
fireplaces or woodburning stoves; two with tubs for
two. Complimentary full breakfast served in the
inn's restaurant or in your room. Restaurant serves
fixed-price dinners. Spa. No handicapped access.
Two-night minimum stay on weekends; three-night
minimum stay during holiday periods. Smoking is
allowed in cottages. Moderate to expensive.

Getting There

From Highway 101 at Petaluma, exit at Washington
Street and drive west through town toward the coast.
At Highway 1, turn north and follow to Gualala.
Inn is two miles north of town on right. From High-
way 101 at Santa Rosa, exit at River Road (becomes
Highway 116) and drive west toward the coast. At
Highway 1 south of Jenner, turn north and follow
to Gualala. Inn is two miles north of town on right.
Check in at the main building. The innkeeper will
provide you with a map to your cottage.

St. Orres

Gualala

$\mathcal{T}$he artful Russian-style domes and weathered redwood façade of St. Orres are a familiar sight to motorists passing through Gualala on coastal Highway 1. Unbeknownst to many travelers, however, is the collection of romantic cottages that are all but hidden from view among the trees behind the main building. So remote are these jewels that you'll have to drive to your cottage after checking in at the registration desk.

Rooms for Romance

The cottages at St. Orres are clustered in two areas. The Meadows, located upslope from the main building, consists of three cottages. Our favorite here is Tree House (mid $100 range), a remote retreat that oozes romance. Guests have an ocean view from the private deck, from the couch in the separate sitting area, and from the queen-sized bed. In the tiled bathroom we discovered a deep soaking tub for two. Tree House also boasts a woodburning stove, lots of windows, and a large skylight.

Rose Cottage (low to mid $100 range), which offers the best ocean view, has an elevated bedroom and a sitting area furnished with a woodburning stove and sofabed.

The rustic Wildflower cottage (under $100) has a loft with a double bed, a woodburning stove, and a seductive outdoor hot water shower with a forest view.

Just north of the main building is the other compound, called Creekside, where guests have use of a facility equipped with a spa, sauna, and sun deck. Seven cottages dot the forested grounds here.

Creekside's two most popular cottages are Pine Haven (upper $100 range) and Sequoia (mid $100 range). Pine Haven, the largest of the cottages, borrows its distinctive architecture from the Russian-style main building. Inside the domed cottage is a tiled breakfast area with an ocean view, an attractive woodburning fireplace, and a wet bar. There are two redwood decks.

Sequoia, the resort's most oft-requested cottage, contains an elevated bedroom alcove illuminated by a skylight. The bathroom holds a deep soaking tub for two. You'll also be treated to an ocean view and a spacious deck.

Offered for less than $100 at the time of our visit, the rustic and simple Fern Canyon is one of the north coast's best bargains. This cozy cottage, with a double bed, also features two redwood decks.

The main hotel building holds eight small upstairs rooms that share three bathrooms. We do not recommend these accommodations for romantic getaways.

The highly acclaimed dining room at St. Orres, which is open to the public, serves three-course dinners priced, at the time of our visit, at around $30.

North Coast Country Inn

34591 South Highway 1
Gualala, CA 95445
Telephone: (707) 884-4537 or
toll-free: (800) 959-4537

Four rooms, each with private bath, woodburning
fireplace, kitchenette, and deck. Complimentary full
breakfast delivered to your room. Spa. No handicapped
access. Smoking is not permitted. Two-night minimum
stay required during weekends; three-night minimum
stay required during holiday periods. Moderate.

Getting There
From Highway 101 at Petaluma, exit at Washington
Street and drive west through town toward the coast.
At Highway 1, turn north and follow to Gualala. Inn is
four miles north of town. From Highway 101 at Santa
Rosa, exit at River Road, which becomes Highway 116,
and drive west toward the coast. At Highway 1 south
of Jenner, turn north and follow to Gualala. Inn is four
miles north of town on right.

North Coast Country Inn

Gualala

*A*fter visits to the seductive Seacliff and Whale Watch Inn for our first volume of weekends for two, and more recently to St. Orres, we were fairly convinced that we had exhausted the romantic potential of tiny Gualala (pronounced *wa-LA-la*). Then we happened upon Loren and Nancy Flanagan's enchanting North Coast Country Inn north of town and concluded that, with all due respect to Mendocino, Gualala is the north coast's most romantic destination.

This redwood-sided inn, nearly hidden behind lush foliage on the east side of Highway 1,

is a real charmer, boasting a definite pride of ownership. Converted a few years ago from an art gallery, the four-room hostelry overlooks the ocean and is within ear shot of a convivial sea lion rookery. The playful barking in the distance is but one of the inn's appealing characteristics.

Rooms for Romance

Each of the four rooms, offered in the low to mid $100 range, is a winner, but we have our own favorites. The most popular is Gallery, a favorite among honeymooners. French doors open to a very private retreat with a skylit, queen-sized four-poster bed, woodburning fireplace, and kitchenette. A sheltered private deck out front can be enjoyed year round. This room does not offer an ocean view.

Our personal favorite is Sea Urchin, a large bright corner room with a vine-draped side deck. This room, which offers just a peek of ocean, is equipped with two comfortable chairs, a handcrafted tester bed, a brick fireplace, and a kitchenette. Above is an open-beamed ceiling with exposed wooden trusses. The adjacent Quilt and Aquitaine rooms are similarly equipped and have ocean views.

A romantic bonus are two lovely retreats maintained on the upper part of the inn's property. One wooded path leads up a hillside to a secluded hot tub under the trees, while another trail ends at a little glen with a quaint gazebo and sitting deck.

Wharfmaster's Inn

785 Port Road
Point Arena, CA 95468
Telephone: (707) 882-3171 or
toll free: (800) 932-4031

Twenty-four rooms, each with private bath and tub for two; twenty-two rooms with fireplaces. Amenities include complimentary bottle of local wine. Complimentary full breakfast served in your room. Handicapped access. Smoking is permitted on decks only. Two-night minimum stay required during holiday periods. Moderate to expensive.

Getting There
From Highway 101 four miles north of Santa Rosa, exit at River Road and drive west for twenty-seven miles to Jenner. Head north on Highway 1 and drive sixty miles to Point Arena. Turn left on Iverson Road (turns into Port Road) and drive one and a half miles to inn. Point Arena is one-hundred-forty miles north of San Francisco and one-hundred-sixty miles from Sacramento.

Wharfmaster's Inn

Point Arena

*I*n the mid-1880s, an ornate, Eastlake-style Victorian home was built on a hillside overlooking the sea for the wharfmaster of the Point Arena Cove. Today the landmark residence is the centerpiece of Wharfmaster's Inn, one of the secret romantic retreats we discovered along the rugged Mendocino coast.

A cluster of contemporary-style, two-story buildings, each painted brown with white trim, sits adjacent to and above the original home, whose interior is pictured here. Some of the inn's rooms, offered in the low $100 range, offer hillside and/or courtyard views; others, priced from the mid $100 range and up, offer dramatic ocean vistas.

Rooms for Romance

The renovated former home of the wharfmaster's family now boasts luxury accommodations that can sleep two to four couples.

A two-room suite here (low $200 range), which can be closed off from the rest of the house, has a tiny bathroom placed between the bedroom and sitting room. The bedroom features an antique bed covered with a lush, cream-colored spread, while the sitting room contains a large whirlpool tub for two surrounded by tile and mirrors. Doors open onto an oceanside deck.

The Lookout wing offers spectacular ocean views. Lookout Room C, for example, has a queen-sized four-poster bed placed beside a glass door and ocean-view deck. With rose-colored carpet, dried flowers, and antiques, the room's interior strikes a pleasant contrast to the rustic looking façade. There's no reason to stray farther than the four walls here. Simply light a fire, open the door, lie back in the whirlpool tub for two, and listen to the everpresent sound of the surf.

Just below the hillside inn is a commercial building that, at the time of our visit, housed a pizza parlor and a seafood restaurant.

Fensalden Inn

33810 Navarro Ridge Road
Albion, CA 95410
Telephone: (707) 937-4042 or
toll-free: (800) 959-3850

Eight rooms, each with private bath; four with
fireplaces. Complimentary full breakfast served
at communal table. Complimentary appetizers
served each afternoon. Handicapped access.
Smoking is not permitted. Two-night minimum
stay required during weekends; three-night
minimum stay required during holiday periods.
Moderate.

Getting There
From Highway 101 at Cloverdale, drive west on
Highway 128 toward the coast. At Highway 1,
turn north and drive two miles to Navarro Ridge
Road. Turn right and drive one-quarter-of-a-mile
to inn on left.

Fensalden Inn

Albion

$\mathcal{T}$he years have been kind to stately Fensalden, a former way station and tavern where stagecoach passengers traveling between Northern California's coastal and valley communities cooled their heels over a hundred years ago. Evidence of shotgun blasts in the sturdy, hundred-year-old ceiling attests to the intemperate goings on during the old days when Albion was a remote outpost.

Fortunately, the wild times are over. It's much calmer here these days, with coastal quiet interrupted only by whispering couples and flickering fires.

Rooms for Romance

Of the five homespun rooms within the handsome main house, we recommend the second-floor Pearl Suite (low $100 range), a spacious love nest tucked under the eaves with separate sitting and sleeping rooms and a fireplace. The east and west views include open pasture lands that sweep to the ocean.

An enclosed antique water tower holds two other charming rooms. Cypress (low $100 range) has a cathedral ceiling and a corner brick fireplace. Three tall windows overlook cypress trees that frame an ocean view.

The inn's most expensive room (low to mid $100 range) is the Captain's Walk Suite, where massive tank support beams figure into the room's design. A curving wooden stairway leads to a spacious sleeping loft with windows that face east and west. This room also has a fireplace and a full kitchen.

The most unusual accommodation on the property is a remote bungalow (low $100 range) situated a few hundred yards from the main house. Resembling a relic from the psychedelic sixties, this eclectic, freestanding hideaway features lots of intriguing angles, big wooden beams, and windows. It's equipped with a queen-sized bed (there's also a loft with a twin bed), a love seat facing a woodburning stove, and a private bathroom with a bathtub and separate shower. The full kitchen features a redwood burl counter top. If you enjoy a rustic environment and are open to a different overnight experience, you'll get a kick out of the bungalow. If your tastes are more traditional, you probably won't.

A mowed path through Fensalden's twenty acres offers soothing ocean vistas.

Agate Cove Bed-and-Breakfast Inn

11201 Lansing Street
Mendocino, CA 95460
Telephone: (707) 937-0551

Ten rooms, each with private bath; nine with fireplaces and two with tubs for two. Amenities include morning newspaper brought to your door. Complimentary full breakfast served at communal tables. Smoking is not permitted. Two-night minimum stay required during weekends; three-night minimum stay required during holiday periods. Moderate to expensive.

Getting There
From northbound Highway 1 in Mendocino, turn left at Lansing Street (third exit in town) and follow to inn driveway on left.

Agate Cove Bed-and-Breakfast Inn

Mendocino

*C*harming cottages overlooking the churning Pacific, white Adirondack chairs on the lawn facing the water, beautiful sunsets, fireplaces to warm your toes . . . Agate Cove is quintessential Mendocino.

Consisting primarily of quaint blue-and-white cottages (some of them are duplex units) with simple but comfortable furnishings, the inn occupies a gentle hill just a stone's throw from the ocean cliffs. The white-water and blue-water views from this property are among the most dramatic we've found.

Rooms for Romance

We have four favorite cottages. The best of the bunch are Emerald and Obsidian (high $100 range), whose picture windows and outdoor decks have dramatic views of the Mendocino headlands and the ocean. These also have nicely dressed, king-sized four-poster beds, woodburning stoves, and in the bathrooms, huge tubs for two (with bubble bath) that double as spacious showers with his and hers spigots.

Garnet and Topaz (mid to upper $100 range) are situated off by themselves and are similarly furnished with king-sized four-poster beds and woodburning stoves. These cottages, which also afford good ocean views, are equipped with showers for two.

The property is situated between Highway 1 and the ocean cliffs, and the sound of traffic can be heard. The noise subsides significantly after 5 p.m. when the logging trucks stop running. The Zircon, Moonstone, and Topaz cottages back up to the highway. The Garden room has neither an ocean view nor outside seating.

A grand breakfast, cooked on a woodburning stove, is served at communal tables in a stunning picture-windowed breakfast room in the inn's main building.

REED MANOR

Palette Drive
Mendocino, CA 95460
Telephone: (707) 937-5446

Five rooms, each with private bath, gas fireplace, tub for two, television with videocassette player, stereo radio, refrigerator, and telephone with answering machine. Complimentary continental breakfast placed in your room's refrigerator prior to check-in. No handicapped access. Smoking is not permitted indoors. Two-night minimum stay required on weekends; three-night minimum stay during holiday periods. Expensive to deluxe.

Getting There
From northbound Highway 1 in Mendocino, turn left on Little Lake Road. Turn right on Lansing Street and right on Palette Drive to inn driveway on right.

A note to our readers:
Because at one time during our travels Reed Manor was for sale, we identified a romantic alternative should you not find the welcome mat out here. Mendocino Hotel & Garden Suites offers a couple of appealing lodging alternatives. The rooms in the landmark hotel building on Main Street contain rich Victorian-style furnishings, and several have ocean and/or village views. Keep in mind, however, that some of the rooms share bathrooms. Deluxe rooms with private contemporary baths run from around $100 to around $200. Behind the hotel are the garden suites, modeled after an adjacent historic residence. These accommodations combine contemporary amenities with garden views. For reservation information, call the Mendocino Hotel at (707) 937-1511, or toll free: (800) 548-0513.

Reed Manor

Mendocino

*I*n a laid-back community where homespun country inns are de rigueur, Reed Manor is an anomaly. Without question Mendocino's premier luxury inn, the manor tempts guests with the ultimate in romantic splendor.

Commanding a lofty hillside perch overlooking the village, Reed Manor is a contemporary-style retreat that resembles a grand residence.

Rooms for Romance

If your heart is set on an ocean view, only the second-floor Napoleon or Majestic Rose will do. In our opinion, Napoleon is the most romantic guest room in Mendocino. This elegant hideaway offers a canopied king-sized bed and a small covered balcony overlooking the village and ocean. A two-sided gas fireplace is visible from the bedroom as well as from the seductive bathroom, which contains an oval tub for two and a spacious shower with a vertical set of water jets. There's also a television in the bathroom. Although this room carries a hefty rate of around $300 per night, it has all the ingredients for a romantic experience you'll not soon forget.

Next door is Majestic Rose, a two-room suite fit for a king, and carrying a king-sized rate in the mid $300 range.

The least expensive room in the manor (upper $100 range) is Imperial Garden, a comparatively small room that exudes a somewhat formal ambience. Guests here have a private, elevated outdoor deck (no ocean view).

Morning Glory, one of the inn's most popular rooms, attracts the morning sun and carries a rate in the mid $200 range. The centerpiece here is an oval-shaped spa tub that can be curtained off from the rest of the room, if desired. The private deck is equipped with a high-powered telescope for village viewing.

Josephine's Garden (around $200) is a tastefully wallpapered, first-floor end unit with a spacious outdoor deck (no ocean view).

Avalon House

561 Stewart Street
Fort Bragg, CA 95437
Telephone: (707) 964-5555 or
toll-free: (800) 964-5556

Six rooms, each with private bath; four rooms with
gas fireplaces and four rooms with spa tubs for
two. Complimentary full breakfast served at communal table. No handicapped access. Smoking is
not permitted. Two-night minimum stay required
during weekends; two-to-three-night minimum
stay required during holiday periods. Moderate.

Getting There
From northbound Highway 1 in Fort Bragg (eight
miles north of Mendocino), turn left on Fir Street
and left on Stewart Street. Inn is on the corner.

Avalon House

Fort Bragg

*F*ort Bragg certainly lacks the seacoast charm and romantic appeal of Mendocino, its neighbor to the south, but we're occasionally asked about suitable accommodations here, especially by couples planning a railroad excursion into the coastal redwoods aboard the popular Skunk train. Avalon House, located only about two blocks from the Skunk depot, fits the bill.

The venerable three-story home, built around the turn of the century as a wedding present from a father to his son, sits on a corner in a modest neighborhood just west of the Fort Bragg downtown area.

Rooms for Romance

The Yellow and Blue rooms (low $100 range) on the third floor receive our highest marks. The Yellow Room is furnished with a bent-willow canopied, queen-sized bed and two matching chairs also fashioned from willow. A long spa tub big enough for two is situated in the room, as is a gas fireplace. You can spy the ocean over Fort Bragg rooftops from a spacious and private deck.

The ocean is also visible from the adjacent Blue Room, whose centerpiece is a handcrafted willow, sleigh-style queen-sized bed. This room has a spa tub and a gas fireplace as well.

The Gray and Pink rooms, two cozy retreats on the second floor, are offered for around $100. The Peach Room (less than $100) is the inn's smallest.

The very private Quilt Room has a private entrance off the garden.

Carter House Cottage

301 L Street (check-in address)
Eureka, CA 95501
Telephone: (707) 445-1390

Three rooms, each with private bath, spa tub for
two, and television with videocassette player; two
with fireplaces. Complimentary full breakfast served
across the street in the Hotel Carter. Complimentary
tea, cookies, and wine served every afternoon. No
handicapped access. Smoking is not permitted.
Two-night minimum stay required during weekends
and holiday periods. Moderate to expensive.

Getting There
From Highway 101 in downtown Eureka, drive
west on L Street through Old Town and check
in at Hotel Carter, Third and L streets.

Carter House Cottage

Eureka

*E*ureka innkeeper Mark Carter has done it again with the renovation of this late-1800s, vintage stick-style Victorian, the third in the Carter family's romantic "neighborhood" of Old Town Eureka properties.

The single-story, yellow-and-white home-turned-inn sits in the shadow of the ornate country inn that Mark personally handcrafted, and just up the street is the three-story, Victorian-style hotel also built by the innkeeper. These two properties are featured in our first volume.

Rooms for Romance

The exterior is nineteenth-century Victorian, but the cottage's interior boasts contemporary conveniences that the original residents couldn't have even dreamed about. There are only three rooms in the inn, and each is trimmed with rich woods and marble, and equipped with halogen lights and bathrooms with marble-faced spa tubs for two. Fine modern art decorates the walls.

Rooms 1 and 3 (mid $100 range) have woodburning fireplaces and queen-sized beds, while Room 2 (low $100 range), a somewhat smaller retreat, holds a double bed.

There's also a common parlor with a fireplace and a contemporary kitchen available for guest use. A complimentary full breakfast, one of the north state's best, is served in the hotel.

The Wine Country

DAYTIME DIVERSIONS

The art of winemaking complements an impressive exhibition of contemporary art at the Hess Collection winery. You'll enjoy the woodsy drive west into the mountains along Redwood Road from Napa to this unusual backroad winery and gallery.

At lunchtime, pick up picnic fixings at Oakville Grocery on Highway 29 in Oakville, and drive up Oakville Grade to Vichon Winery, site of one of the valley's preeminent picnic spots. Don't forget to first obtain permission at the tasting room to use a table.

The tram ride up the mountain to Sterling Vineyards winery is worth taking, at least once. At the top you'll hopefully be able to find a tasting room table for two and enjoy a glass of Sterling wine. For a more intimate winery experience, call ahead to Deer Park Winery, (707) 963-5411, and arrange a visit to this hidden stone-walled cellar.

For a different experience, consider a mud bath together. Among the dozen or so spas in Calistoga is Indian Springs Spa and Resort, in operation for more than a century. It offers mud and mineral baths and massages, as well as use of its heated outdoor swimming pool.

TABLES FOR TWO

Applewood, an Estate Inn (described in this section), whose dining room is open for dinners only, serves multicourse, candlelit meals that earn consistent raves. Our innkeepers recommend Tre Scalini (241 Healdsburg Avenue) just off the plaza in Healdsburg; La Gare (Railroad Square, Wilson Street, Santa Rosa); Calistoga Inn (1250 Lincoln Avenue, Calistoga); Showley's at Miramonte (1327 Railroad Avenue, St. Helena); French Laundry (6640 Washington Street, Yountville); and Chanterelle (804 First Street, Napa). Our Napa Valley favorite remains Tra Vigne (1050 Charter Oak at Highway 29, St. Helena).

AFTER HOURS

Savor the valley view with a glass of wine from the hillside terrace of Auberge du Soleil above the Silverado Trail in Rutherford. It doesn't get much more romantic than this.

CHURCHILL MANOR

485 Brown Street
Napa, CA 94559
Telephone: (707) 253-7733

Ten rooms, each with private bath and telephone;
three with fireplaces; one with spa tub for two.
Complimentary full breakfast served in dining room
at tables for two or four, or can be taken to your
room. Complimentary evening wine and cheese and
afternoon cookies served daily. Bicycles, including
two tandems, available for free guest use. Handicapped access. Smoking is not permitted. Guests
staying on a Saturday night must stay a second
night. Moderate to expensive.

Getting There
From Highway 29, exit at First Street and follow
downtown Napa signs onto Second Street. Turn
right on Jefferson Street (first stoplight) and drive
two blocks to Oak Street. Turn left on Oak and
drive seven blocks to Brown Street. The inn is on
the southwest corner of Oak and Brown streets.

Churchill Manor

Napa

*D*on't assume that a romantic night in the Napa Valley will necessarily strain your pocketbook. We discovered this grand bed-and-breakfast inn in Napa's historic residential section offering some rooms at less than $100.

You'll fall in love with this stately manse the moment you walk through the garden and step up to the Southern-style veranda that sweeps around the front of the home. Few bed-and-breakfast inns we've visited offer a more pleasant public area.

Rooms for Romance

The aptly named Bordello Room (mid $100 range) is described by the innkeepers as "naughty but nice." Inside this third-floor retreat is a king-sized brass bed flanked by a mirrored, antique French armoire. Step inside the bathroom and you'll find a red-and-black spa tub for two.

If a clawfoot tub (big enough for two in a pinch) in your bedroom sounds appealing, ask about Rose's Room and Victoria's Room. In each of these rooms the tub has been placed romantically in a windowed corner near the bed and fireplace. These rooms are offered in the low to mid $100 range.

At the time of our visit, about half the rooms—these admittedly smaller—carried rates of around $100 or less. Among the bargains was Robert's Room on the third floor, where a twisted wood, queen-sized canopied bed is the centerpiece. The bathroom has an antique tub-and-shower combination.

Similarly priced are Amy's Room, with a queen-sized brass bed and a bathroom with a tiled shower, and Granny's Room, furnished with a queen-sized bed and wicker furnishings. These cozy rooms are also tucked on the quiet third floor.

In our opinion, the first-floor Garden Room is a bit too close to the inn's dining room.

Travelers should be aware that many couples choose the gorgeous grounds of Churchill Manor to exchange vows, and wedding parties sometimes book the entire inn during weekend periods from May through October.

Blue Violet Mansion

443 Brown Street
Napa, CA 94559
Telephone: (707) 253-2583

Seven rooms, each with private bath; five with gas fireplaces; three with tubs for two. Full breakfast can be taken at a communal table or in your room. Innkeepers serve private, gourmet, multicourse dinners in your room at extra charge. No handicapped access. Smoking is not permitted. Two-night minimum stay required during weekends from June through October and holiday periods. Moderate to expensive.

Getting There
From Highway 29 in Napa, exit east at Imola Street and drive into town. Turn left on Coombs Street and drive a half-mile to Laurel Street and turn right. Drive one block to Brown Street and turn left to inn.

Blue Violet Mansion

Napa

*T*n Napa, the quality of older homes-turned-inns is as diverse as the region's wines, from the inexpensive generics to aging beauties waiting to be savored. Tucked away on a quiet residential street a short walk from downtown Napa, Blue Violet Mansion is the cabernet of Napa Valley's Victorian bed-and-breakfast inns.

This hundred-year-old gem had operated as a chopped-up apartment building before Bob and Kathy Morris bought the home and began restoration in 1990. After rehabilitating the structure, the innkeepers filled the public and guest rooms with a trove of exquisite furnishings ranging from Victoriana to contemporary pieces. Bob, an art collector, has lavished every room with tasteful prints, paintings, and sculpture. A whimsical fantasy theme, carried by unicorns, sorcerers, and griffins, is also evident in the public and guest rooms.

Rooms for Romance

A staircase with original leather wainscoting (the home's builder was the creator of a leather tanning method still used) leads to the guest rooms, all clustered on the second floor.

Most tempting is the Blue Violet Room (around $200), which holds the only water bed-type mattress found in any of our destinations. One couple described it as "the bed from heaven." This sunny corner room contains a fireplace and Victorian furniture, and the bathroom, which holds a spa tub for two, is illuminated by a stained-glass window.

A spa tub for two is also found in the Garden Bower Room (high $100 range) where a wall with antique leaded-glass windows separates the bathroom and bedroom.

Queen Victoria's Room (mid to upper $100 range) has a bay-windowed sitting area containing a day bed for relaxing. The ornate carved bed and matching chest and mirror are an antique Flemish wedding set. The room also contains a fireplace, and a clawfoot tub graces the marble-floored bathroom.

Sharing a front-facing balcony with Queen Victoria's Room is His Majesty's Room (high $100 range), whose centerpiece is a king-sized bed with carved headboards. This room also has a bay-windowed sitting area, a fireplace, and a bathroom with a clawfoot tub.

The Rose Room (low to mid $100 range) has a whitewashed, half-canopied pine bed. Hand-painted roses grace both the bed and furniture. In the bathroom are a pedestal sink and a clawfoot tub/shower combination.

The French Boudoir Room (mid $100 range), with its unusual antique bed with square brass rails, is quite small, but the bathroom contains a seductive, forty-inch-deep round spa tub for two.

Facing the back of the house is the Victoriana Suite (high $100 range), which can be split into two lesser-priced rooms when sharing the bath.

La Residence Country Inn

4066 St. Helena Highway North
Napa, CA 94558
Telephone: (707) 253-0337

Twenty rooms, all but two with private baths. Fifteen rooms have woodburning fireplaces and three rooms have soaking tubs for two. Complimentary full breakfast served at tables for two in dining room. Swimming pool and spa. Handicapped access. Smoking is not permitted. Two-night minimum stay required during weekends; three-night minimum stay during holiday periods. Moderate to expensive.

Getting There
From Highway 29 in Napa, drive north and turn right at the first opportunity after the Salvador Avenue traffic light. (There is a restaurant on this corner.) Make another right turn on the drive into the property and follow signs for parking and registration.

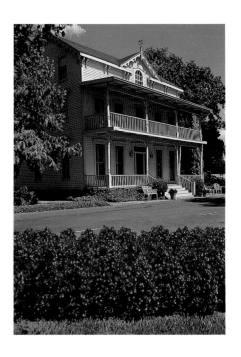

La Residence Country Inn

Napa

*Y*ou may not be familiar with this luxurious small inn, but if you travel Highway 29 out of Napa, it's right under your nose. Tucked among oak trees and gardens along the highway just north of town, La Residence Country Inn ranks among our favorite romantic retreats in Napa Valley.

The inn offers guests something old or something new, but each option is served up with charm and taste. The centerpiece of the two-acre property is a contemporary, two-story, shingled building affectionately referred to as "the barn." Eleven guest rooms and dining facilities comprise the white-trimmed building. A short stroll away is the other half of the inn: an 1870 gothic-revival mansion built for a riverboat captain. The home holds nine rooms and suites.

Rooms for Romance

The most popular room among romantics in-the-know is Room 22 (mid $100 range) in the main building. Decorated in country style, this second-floor room has a brick, woodburning fireplace that's visible from the queen-sized four-poster bed. Two sets of French doors open to a shared balcony. This and the other rooms have bathrooms with tiled tubs and showers.

A grand old oak tree stands just outside the window of Room 25, which holds a queen-sized brass bed. Room 21, accessed via a second-floor deck entry, features a spacious shower built for two in a skylit bathroom.

Rooms 12, 23, and 26 in the main building have deep soaking tubs for two. All rooms in this building feature French and English pine antiques. Double walls between guest rooms and three feet of space between floors ensure your privacy. However, some road noise can be heard.

Rooms in the mansion are spread over three floors and offer a more remote feeling, since they're away from the property's hub. All are furnished with walnut and oak antiques.

Room 1 (high $100 range), a downstairs corner, is equipped with an antique fireplace, a couch, and a queen-sized four-poster bed. In the modern bathroom is a deep tub for two with shower.

Room 6, a second-floor suite, is decorated in rose tones and has a sitting room as well as a balcony with chairs. Rooms 7 and 9 on the third floor share one bathroom.

OAK KNOLL INN

2200 East Oak Knoll Avenue
Napa Valley, CA 94558
Telephone: (707) 255-2200

Four rooms, each with private bath and fireplace.
Complimentary full breakfast served at a communal
table, tables for two, or in your room. Complimentary
early evening wine and hors d'oeuvres. Swimming
pool and spa. No handicapped access. Smoking is not
permitted inside. Guests staying on a Saturday night
must stay a second night. Two-night minimum stay
required during holiday periods. Deluxe.

Getting There
Heading north on Highway 29 from Napa, turn
right on Oak Knoll Avenue (second right turn after
the Salvador Avenue traffic light). Follow Oak Knoll
to Big Ranch Road and turn left. Make a quick right
back onto Oak Knoll to inn on left.

Oak Knoll Inn

Napa Valley

*F*or those who enjoy the environs of central Napa Valley but who prefer country atmosphere to the faster pace of Napa proper, we heartily recommend Oak Knoll Inn.

Situated amid vineyards north of town, the three-and-a-half-acre property offers wide valley views and unobstructed vistas of the eastern mountains, along with amenities like a swimming pool and large communal spa.

Operated as an inn since 1984, Oak Knoll consists of a nicely updated farm house (the parlor area) off of which two field-stone-walled guest room wings were added, forming an L shape. Barbara Passino and John Kuhlmann, husband-and-wife innkeepers since 1992, are responsible for transforming Oak Knoll into one of the valley's preeminent inns.

Rooms for Romance

Rooms at Oak Knoll are among the largest we've sampled in our travels. Each is consistently styled, with plush carpeting, a king-sized brass bed, a woodburning fireplace that can be seen from the bed, and a cozy sitting area with love seat and cushy chairs.

Each room has walls of locally quarried stone and soaring beamed ceilings. Walls between rooms are double-thick, although occasional local traffic can be heard from Oak Knoll Avenue, which runs behind the property. The windowed bathrooms are bright and modern with tub-and-shower combinations in each.

Since guest rooms are entered through French doors facing a common outdoor access, guests in Rooms 2 and 5 must curtain-off the pretty view to ensure privacy. Our personal favorites are Rooms 1 and 6. These two end units offer the most privacy as well as tall, arched windows with vineyard views and small outdoor seating areas. Room rates are in the low to mid $200 range.

In addition to sumptuous accommodations, Oak Knoll treats guests to an outstanding full breakfast.

Forest Manor Bed-and-Breakfast Inn

415 Cold Springs Road
Angwin, CA 94508
Telephone: (707) 965-3538 or
toll-free: (800) 788-0364

Three rooms, each with private bath; two with
woodburning fireplaces. Complimentary full breakfast served at a communal table, on the deck, or in
your room. Billiard table, swimming pool, and spa.
Limited handicapped access. Smoking is not permitted. Two-night minimum stay required during
weekends and holiday periods. Moderate to deluxe.

Getting There
From Highway 29 or the Silverado Trail north of St.
Helena, turn east on Deer Park Road and drive (six
miles from Highway 29) to Cold Springs Road.
Turn right on Cold Springs Road and follow to inn.

Forest Manor Bed-and-Breakfast Inn

Angwin

*B*ecause of our own inconsistent experiences at small bed-and-breakfast inns, we tend to shy away from establishments with only two or three rooms. We made exceptions for only a few, including Forest Manor, because of its superior level of accommodations and professional innkeepers.

Operated for several years by dentist Harold Lambeth and his wife, Corlene, a former teacher, Forest Manor is the most remote of our wine country destinations. The Tudor-style family home occupies a woodsy twenty-acre parcel among oaks and vineyards high above Napa Valley in the tiny community of Angwin. There are no other houses visible from the property.

Rooms for Romance

On the first floor, just inside the entry, is the nine-hundred-square-foot Canterbury Suite (around $200), which includes what was originally the home's large living room. Furnishings here include an ornate, hand-carved teak couch, chairs, and table set arranged around a brick fireplace. The bed is king-sized, and the bathroom contains a shower stall. There's also a separate breakfast room. At the time of our visit, plans called for the addition of an outdoor spa on the deck overlooking the swimming pool.

Our personal favorite is Somerset (around $200), a large and sunny second-floor corner suite facing the rear of the property. A table and chairs sit in a large alcove with five windows, and two comfy chairs are set before a woodburning stove near a king-sized bed. Couples will also savor the spa tub for two. This is one of the wine country's most romantic rooms.

Chelsea (low to mid $100 range) is the other second-floor suite. This one faces the front of the house and contains a queen-sized bed and two chairs. A spiral staircase leads to a third-floor reading loft with love seat.

The inn's backyard contains a swinging chair and an inviting swimming pool with spa. There's a billiard table on the third floor.

THE ELMS

1300 Cedar Street
Calistoga, CA 94515
Telephone: (707) 942-9476 or
toll free: (800) 235-4316

Seven rooms, each with private bath; five with gas
fireplaces. Amenities include bathrobes, coffeemakers,
wine, and chocolates. Complimentary multicourse
breakfast served at communal tables. Complimentary
wine and cheese served each evening. Handicapped
access. Smoking is not permitted. Two-night minimum stay required during weekends; three-night
minimum stay required during some holiday periods.
Moderate to expensive.

Getting There
From northbound Highway 29 in Calistoga, turn
right on Lincoln Avenue and drive two blocks to
Cedar Street. Turn left on Cedar Street. The inn
is on the right adjacent to the park.

The Elms

Calistoga

*F*rom the street, this impressive Victorian—perhaps Calistoga's grandest dame—casts a somewhat formal presence. But step over the threshold and you'll enter a decidedly relaxed, casual environment favored by many wine country visitors.

Operated as a bed-and-breakfast inn for several years by a succession of owners, the mansion was originally the home of a prominent area judge. It's one of few remaining regional examples of the second empire style. The four namesake elm trees out front were planted in 1871, the year the house was built.

Rooms for Romance

Accommodations at The Elms aren't stuffy or formal. A cozy, homespun feel pervades the second and third floor where four bedrooms are located. Palisades Garden (low to mid $100 range), known as the "love nest," has a queen-sized brass bed and offers a view of the mountains. Katherine Hepburn slept here while starring in a movie that featured The Elms.

Our favorite room in the main house is La Chambre (mid $100 range), the second-floor room that faces the elm trees. It features a marble gas fireplace and a queen-sized, lacey canopied bed. A major attraction of this room is the private balcony with a wicker love seat.

Nouveau Dream (mid $100 range) on the second floor has a king-sized bed canopied with Battenburg lace.

Guests in the king-bedded Blithe Spirit must leave their room to access a private bathroom. The skylight is great on those rainy days.

The informal theme is carried to the adjacent carriage house that now houses three rooms. The Honeymoon Cottage (mid to high $100 range), perched on the edge of the wooded Napa River, is a comfy hideaway that contains a queen-sized brass bed, a gas fireplace, a leather sofa, and a kitchenette. In the bathroom is a large shower for two that will beckon both of you. Although not much more than a trickle in summer, the river rushes during winter, providing a very romantic backdrop.

The other outside rooms, Romantic Hideaway and Victorian Fantasy, are small, but feature amenities that include spa tubs, gas fireplaces, and televisions with videocassette players.

Located only a half block from the town's main street, The Elms is within easy walking distance of Calistoga shops, spas, and restaurants.

Foothill House

3037 Foothill Boulevard
Calistoga, CA 94515
Telephone: (707) 942-6933 or
toll-free: (800) 942-6933

Three rooms, each with private bath and woodburning fireplace or woodburning stove, stereo cassette
player, terry robes, small refrigerator, and eating
area. Complimentary full breakfast served communally or delivered to your room. Complimentary
wine and cheese served every afternoon (or brought
to your room). Complimentary cookies placed in
your room in the evening. No handicapped access.
Smoking is not permitted. Two-night minimum stay
required during weekends. Moderate to deluxe.

Getting There
Drive north through Napa Valley on Highway 29.
In Calistoga, the road becomes Highway 128/
Foothill Boulevard. Inn is one-and-a-half miles north
of Calistoga on left.

Foothill House

Calistoga

*I*t took a visit to Foothill House outside Calistoga to remind us how romantic outdoor spaces and sounds can be when combined with the right amount of indoor intimacy. The designers of this retreat artfully incorporated the beauty of nature into the overall scheme, especially in two of the suites.

The smallest of our wine country destinations, Foothill House is a country farm house that's been updated and converted into a luxury inn with but three rooms. Part of the main house now serves as a gathering place that includes a pretty glass-enclosed dining area facing the backyard and gazebo.

Rooms for Romance

We've yet to discover a California guest room that rivals—in terms of romantic appeal—the freestanding Quail's Roost. Situated at the top of the property, this striking contemporary cottage has it all: a king-sized four-poster bed, a raised, double-walled woodburning fireplace that can be viewed from bed and bath, a spacious sitting area with a cushy couch and entertainment center, a romantic reading nook with daybed, a kitchen (you may not want to leave for dinner), and woodsy views from the windows.

The glorious bathroom contains not only a spa tub for two but a shower for two. The glass wall in the shower looks out on your private waterfall. French doors open to a private patio. The rate is in the low to mid $200 range, but this ultimate honeymoon haven is well worth saving your pennies for.

Our other favorite here is the Evergreen Suite (upper $100 range), a four-hundred-square-foot stunner with a queen-sized canopied bed, a reading alcove with daybed, a love seat facing a brick fireplace, and a small table and chairs set placed next to a large picture window. Outside is your enclosed private deck with a gently running fountain. Although the spa tub in the bathroom was designed for one, with a bit of maneuvering . . .

The inn's third room, the Foothill Lupine Suite (mid $100 range) is situated next to the office and faces the parking area. It's a deep room—a bit on the dark side—with a queen-sized four-poster bed near the sliding glass door, a love seat and small table and chairs at the center, and a woodburning stove at the far end. The bathroom is equipped with a tub-and-shower combination.

Kenwood Inn

10400 Sonoma Highway
Kenwood, CA 95452
Telephone: (707) 833-1293

Twelve rooms, each with private bath, fireplace, stereo cassette deck, and spa tub for two. Complimentary full breakfast served at tables for two in dining room. Complimentary bottle of wine provided on arrival. Swimming pool. No handicapped access. Smoking is not permitted. Two-night minimum stay required during weekends and holiday periods. Expensive to deluxe.

Getting There
From Sonoma, drive north on Highway 12 to inn on left in Kenwood. From Highway 101 in Santa Rosa, drive south on Highway 12 to inn on right in Kenwood.

Kenwood Inn

Kenwood

A sublime Italian-style pensione tucked into the Valley of the Moon only about forty-five minutes from San Francisco, Kenwood Inn is arguably Sonoma County's most romantic destination.

Terry and Roseann Grimm, longtime owners of San Francisco's Anchor Oyster Bar, are the masterful creators of this romantic haven. Roseann is the restaurateur while Terry, a former builder who added the guest rooms, handles innkeeping duties.

Rooms for Romance

Each of the rooms we inspected were of honeymoon quality. In fact, the friends we dispatched initially to investigate the inn's romantic potential were so enamored they ended up staying an extra night.

Room 6 (low $200 range), known as the Honeymoon Suite, is set privately on the second floor. The suite holds a canopied bed and is decorated in a workable combination of mango, burgundy, and black. A covered balcony overlooks the garden area.

Room 3, which has a private patio and a separate garden entrance, is equipped with a living room fireplace. Room 4, which backs onto a wooded area, also has a fireplace. These rooms are offered in the upper $100 range.

At the time of our visit, Terry and Roseann were in the process of creating eight additional guest rooms and a six-room spa, with plans for a full dining room offering dinner service.

The Gables Bed-and-Breakfast Inn

4257 Petaluma Hill Road
Santa Rosa, CA 95404
Telephone: (707) 585-7777

Seven rooms, each with private bath; three with woodburning stoves or fireplaces. Complimentary full breakfast served at communal table or in your room. Complimentary wine and cheese served every afternoon. No handicapped access. Smoking is not permitted. Two-night minimum stay required during weekends; three-night minimum stay required during some holiday weekends. Moderate to expensive.

Getting There
From Highway 101 in Santa Rosa, exit east at Rohnert Park Expressway to Petaluma Hill Road. Turn north on Petaluma Hill Road to inn on left.

The Gables Bed-and-Breakfast Inn

Santa Rosa

*W*e've toured gingerbread-bedecked Victorians from Ferndale to Pacific Grove, but nothing quite compares with this unusually-styled inn situated, in of all places, Santa Rosa.

This rare example of high-Victorian gothic revival architecture is a town landmark, most noted for fifteen steep gables—hence the inn's name—and numerous striking keyhole-shaped and shuttered windows. Originally the family home of a successful dairyman, the Gables sits on three-and-a-half acres in the country just outside Santa Rosa.

Rooms for Romance

For couples who like to be away from it all, our top pick here is William and Mary's Cottage (high $100 range), a separate retreat set away from the main house near Taylor Creek. It's equipped with a woodburning stove, a kitchenette, and a spa tub for two.

In the main house are six rooms and suites, all appointed with antique furniture, brass beds with goose-down comforters, and fresh flowers.

The Parlor Suite (mid $100 range) holds a king-sized bed and a fireplace.

The largest room in the house is the Garden View Suite (low $100 range), with a queen-sized bed and a twin bed set in a small alcove.

A nice redwood deck overlooks an expansive back lawn, and a quaint foot bridge crosses Taylor Creek to a meadow.

The Farmhouse Inn

7871 River Road
Forestville, CA 95436
Telephone: (707) 887-3300 or
toll-free in California: (800) 464-6642

Eight rooms and suites, each with private bath;
most with spa tubs for two, saunas, and fireplaces.
Complimentary full breakfast served in common
dining room, or continental breakfast available in
your room. Complimentary tea served every afternoon. Swimming pool, restaurant with seasonal
hours. Handicapped access. Smoking is not permitted. Two-night minimum stay required during weekends and holiday periods. Moderate to expensive.

Getting There
From Highway 101 north of Santa Rosa, take the
River Road/Guerneville exit and drive west on River
Road to inn on left near the intersection of Wohler
Road and River Road.

The Farmhouse Inn

Forestville

A discovery tour of Sonoma County's small backroad wineries yielded an unexpected treasure when we came, quite by accident, upon The Farmhouse Inn tucked in a lush setting along scenic River Road.

Among the region's lesser-known hideaways, the six-acre estate has a long history, dating back to the 1870s when the Johnson family built a country farmhouse here. The renovated home today holds the inn's common rooms, including a restaurant. Across the driveway are the cozy guest cottages with pitched roofs and chimneys, arranged in a motel-style row.

Rooms for Romance

Obviously created by a savvy romantic, the inn's eight rooms and suites boast more seductive features than most of our recommended destinations.

Rooms 1 through 4 (low $100 range) feature queen-sized beds, fireplaces, and bathrooms equipped with spa tubs for two. Rooms 1, 2, and 4 also have seating areas; rooms 1, 3, and 4 have saunas. Room 8 (mid $100 range) has a king-sized platform bed, a sauna, a spa tub for two, a fireplace, and a seating area. The day bed in Room 5 makes into a pair of twins.

The inn's most spacious accommodations, offered in the mid to upper $100 range, are suites 6 and 7. These romantic retreats boast living rooms with couches that convert to double beds, fireplaces, separate bedrooms with king-sized beds, large saunas, and spa tubs for two.

All rooms contain a mix of American and European antiques and feature lighting controlled by dimmer switches. There's also a swimming pool on-site.

Applewood, an Estate inn

13555 Highway 116
Pocket Canyon, CA 95446
Telephone: (707) 869-9093

Ten rooms, each with private bath. Complimentary full breakfast served at tables for two or four. Dining room (dinners only), swimming pool, and spa. Handicapped access. Smoking is not permitted. Two-night minimum stay required during weekends; three-night minimum stay required during holiday periods. Moderate to expensive.

Getting There
From Highway 101 two miles north of Santa Rosa, take River Road/Guerneville exit and drive west fourteen miles to Highway 116. Turn left and cross the Russian River, and drive a half-mile to inn on left.

Applewood, an Estate Inn

Pocket Canyon

After years of unsuccessful searching, we had almost given up hope of finding a suitably romantic retreat in the Russian River region. Then we followed up on an effusive review of a meal enjoyed at Applewood, an Estate Inn, and hit the jackpot.

Tucked into a lush hillside among the redwoods, this 1920s, mission-style mansion made an easy transition from home to a combination inn and restaurant. Rooms don't have the retrofitted look of those in some homes-turned-inns, and the dining room and public areas are generous and inviting.

A previous owner created ten guest rooms in anticipation of opening an inn, but funds ran short and the grand old home sat vacant for a time during the mid-1980s. That's when San Franciscans Jim Caron and Darryl Notter happened by while on a wine country vacation in 1985. The two bought the place and furnished the guest rooms with a mix of contemporary and antique furnishings.

Jim, who has become an accomplished chef during his innkeeping tenure, is primarily responsible for the superb candlelit dinners served (at extra charge) at Applewood. Guests are treated to a full breakfast served at tables for two or four.

Rooms for Romance

Room 4 (high $100 range) is the inn's largest accommodation. It's furnished with a wicker love seat, two chairs, and a pretty sleigh bed.

If privacy is what you're looking for, Room 10 (high $100 range) is your retreat. Guests step down to the room from the swimming pool area and are greeted by a queen-sized half-canopied bed and love seat. The small bathroom has a tub-and-shower combination.

Just off the inn's living area is Room 8 (mid to upper $100 range) with Louis XV–style furnishings and a lovely covered balcony accessed through French doors. Also off the living room is Room 7, decorated with wall sconces, a pair of chairs, and a queen-sized bed with pine headboard. The pretty view from this room is a bonus.

Room 1 (low $100 range) is stocked with mystery novels and features a private woodsy patio.

Some noise from the adjacent two-lane highway can be heard from the inn (primarily from those rooms facing the road), but traffic dies down at night. Beds are covered with hand-pressed European linens and down comforters.

HOPE-MERRILL HOUSE AND HOPE-BOSWORTH HOUSE

21238 Geyserville Avenue
Geyserville, CA 95441
Telephone: (707) 857-3356 or
toll-free: (800) 825-4BED

Twelve rooms (combined), each with private bath;
four with fireplaces and three with spa tubs for two.
Full breakfast served at communal table. Swimming
pool. Handicapped access. Smoking is not permitted. Two-night minimum stay required during
weekends; three-night minimum stay required during
holiday periods. Moderate to expensive.

Getting There
From Highway 101 north of Santa Rosa, take the
Highway 128 exit and turn right. Turn left on
Geyserville Avenue to the inns on opposite sides
of the street.

Hope-Merrill House and Hope-Bosworth House
Geyserville

A coveted first-place award from the National Trust for Historic Preservation offers but one hint of the innkeeping dedication of Rosalie Hope, proprietor of this pair of landmark homes-turned-inns.

The National Trust award was the culmination of a four-year restoration of the 1870s-era Hope-Merrill House, the more formal of the two properties. Rosalie and her late husband, Bob, lovingly renovated the house in the early 1980s, furnishing its rooms with hand-made silk-screen wallcoverings, exquisite antiques, and lace curtains, while leaving intact the historic curving staircases and intriguing nooks and crannies.

Across the street and behind a picket fence, the Queen Anne–style Hope-Bosworth House is smaller, though equally impressive with original oak grained woodwork, sliding doors, and polished fir floors.

Rooms for Romance
In Hope-Merrill House, room rates are around $100 or in the low $100 range. The downstairs Sterling Room is the largest in the house. Overlooking the swimming pool and gardens, this room features a sitting area, a large woodburning fireplace, a four-poster bed with a lace coverlet, and a private entry off the patio.

Also downstairs, the Peacock Room, decorated in rose hues, offers a fireplace and views of the gazebo and vineyards. The bathroom, set behind French doors, holds a deep marble spa tub for two. The Carpenter Gothic room is also equipped with a spa tub.

Upstairs you'll find the ornate Bradbury Room, with a fireplace and varied patterns of wallpaper peaking to the ceiling. A huge dried rhododendron bouquet serves as the headboard for a queen-sized bed. In the bathroom, dual spigots in the pink-tiled shower represent a crowning romantic touch.

Afternoons often find guests relaxing around the swimming pool or on the wraparound porch with a glass of wine. The pool is available to guests of both properties.

Hope-Bosworth House holds four rooms that are smaller and less expensive than those found across the street. Rooms are priced at around $100 or less. The sunny upstairs Oak Room holds a queen-sized bed positioned diagonally under a ceiling fan. A whirlpool tub is situated in a separate sitting room. A private entrance serves the Sun Porch room on the ground floor.

By the way, Rosalie's popular Coffee Cake Supreme received a best of show award from chef Julia Child and other judges in a bed-and-breakfast bread competition. She proudly shares her recipe with interested guests.

The San Francisco Bay Area

DAYTIME DIVERSIONS

San Francisco, one of the world's most romantic cities, is home to countless places that stir the heart, including the Shakespeare Garden and the Conservatory of Flowers, both in Golden Gate Park. Before a picnic in the park, drop by Molinari's Deli (373 Columbus Avenue) for sandwiches and salads.

A twelve-mile coastal bike trail not open to vehicle traffic is accessible from Half Moon Bay. There's also a trail from Kelly Beach Park that follows the cliffs and dunes to Princeton Harbor. Dunes Beach, also in Half Moon Bay, is a favorite among beach walkers.

There are also beaches, like Heart's Desire, along Tomales Bay and the Point Reyes National Seashore in Marin County. At the venerable Johnson's Oysters (follow signs to Drake's Beach) you can buy oysters in the shell for a beach barbeque. If a coastal walk sounds appealing, ask your innkeeper for a local suggestion. Scores of hiking trails crisscross this region.

TABLES FOR TWO

Pasta Moon (315 Main Street, Half Moon Bay) isn't a quiet, intimate restaurant, but it serves some of the best food along this part of the coast. Across the street is San Benito House, long a Half Moon Bay favorite. Moss Beach Distillery (down the road from Seal Cove Inn) in Moss Beach offers great meals, ocean views, and a convivial atmosphere.

In Marin County, try Manka's (for Czech food) on Argyle Street in Inverness or the Olema Inn on Highway 1 in Olema.

For one of San Francisco's best views and best meals, try McCormick & Kuleto's in Ghirardelli Square (corner of Beach and Larkin streets). Ya Ya Cuisine (1220 Ninth Avenue) serves highly rated Mesopotamian dishes, while stylish Aqua (252 California Street) is a good bet for seafood specialties. Cafe Claude (7 Claude Lane between Bush and Sutter streets) is one of the city's hidden romantic gems. For drinks we can recommend an oceanside table (and oysters, of course) at the Cliff House on Point Lobos Avenue, and the Carnelian Room bar, high atop the Bank of America building at California and Montgomery streets.

The Inn at Saratoga

20645 Fourth Street
Saratoga, CA 95070
Telephone: (408) 867-5020

Forty-six rooms, each with private bath, videocassette player, and patio or deck; six rooms with spa tubs for two. Complimentary continental breakfast served in lobby. Guests have use of the Los Gatos Athletic Club three miles away. Handicapped access. Smoking is allowed. No minimum stay requirements. Expensive to deluxe.

Getting There
From Interstate 280, take the second Route 85 exit, marked Saratoga/Sunnyvale, and turn right on Saratoga/Sunnyvale Road (also known as DeAnza Boulevard). After four miles, turn right on Big Basin Way and drive one-quarter mile to Fourth Street. Turn right on Fourth Street and drive one-half mile to bottom of the hill. Inn is on the right. From Interstate 880, exit to the right at Route 9, marked Los Gatos/Saratoga, follow to Big Basin Way, and turn left. Drive one-quarter mile to Fourth Street. Turn right on Fourth Street and drive one-half mile to bottom of the hill. Inn is on the right.

The Inn at Saratoga

Saratoga

espite the frenetic pulse of Silicon Valley, which beats only a few miles away, the village of Saratoga has managed to retain a romantic and charming ambience. You won't find tacky souvenir shops or noisy taverns. Instead, art galleries, boutiques, and upscale restaurants abound.

While most Bay Area motorists breeze in only for a few hours of shopping and maybe a meal or two, a night here can be an enchanting experience, especially if your home base is The Inn at Saratoga.

Nestled beside Wildwood Park and Saratoga Creek beneath sycamore, maple, and eucalyptus trees, the inn holds forty-six rooms, all with floor-to-ceiling windows that take advantage of the wooded view. The five-story structure doesn't resemble a typical country inn, nor can it be accurately described as a motel or hotel; it's an attractive hybrid.

Rooms for Romance

The least expensive rooms (those starting in the mid $100 range) are clean and contemporary but fairly standard from a romantic's perspective. We recommend one of the six deluxe, king-bedded rooms with spa tubs for two ($200 to mid $200 range). The deep, gently sloping tubs here are even equipped with plastic pillows for the ultimate in relaxation.

Among the most romantic are the Olivia DeHavilland and Joan Fontaine suites, both of which have bathrooms that feature a television, a heated towel rack, double vanities, and a separate shower.

A night at the inn is an especially romantic complement to one of the many concerts held at the beautiful Paul Masson Winery located nearby.

Mill Rose Inn

615 Mill Street
Half Moon Bay, CA 94019
Telephone: (415) 726-9794 or
toll-free: (800) 900-7673

Six rooms, each with private bath, television, videocassette player, and cassette deck; five with gas fireplace. Amenities include sandals and kimonos, morning newspaper, and complimentary refreshments. Complimentary full champagne breakfast served at tables for two or in your room. Complimentary wine and refreshments served each afternoon. Spa. No handicapped access. Smoking is not permitted. Two-night minimum stay required during weekends and holiday periods. Expensive to deluxe.

Getting There
From Highway 1 in Half Moon Bay, drive east on Highway 92 to Main Street and turn right. Follow Main Street to Mill Street and turn right. Inn is two blocks on right. Half Moon Bay is approximately twenty-six miles south of San Francisco, thirty-nine miles from San Jose, and one-hundred-ten miles from Sacramento.

Mill Rose Inn

Half Moon Bay

*I*n our original Northern California guide, the town of Half Moon Bay was unfortunately not represented. Motivated by our own wanderlust and by requests from traveling romantics for overnight recommendations here, we've scouted out a trio of destinations. Those looking to make magical memories in a luxurious setting won't be disappointed with Mill Rose Inn, which in our opinion offers Half Moon Bay's most romantic lodgings.

A white picket fence and an explosion of color from the inn's gardens greet visitors to this charming property set in a neighborhood of modest homes just a couple of blocks from Main Street.

Guests are received in a quaint, historic cottage that houses the common rooms and two guest rooms. A two-story annex with gables and window boxes was added a few years ago and brought four more tantalizing rooms to the inn.

Rooms for Romance

The Mill Rose is one of the coastal area's most exquisitely decorated inns, and the rooms here boast lush window treatments, fireplaces with hand-painted tiles, and tasteful wallpaper.

Two rooms are located just off the reception area in the cottage. Bordeaux Rose (mid $200 range), favored by honeymooners, pampers guests with a queen-sized lace-canopied bed. The bathroom has a marble shower and a spa tub for two that is framed by mirrors and stained glass.

Baroque Rose (mid $100 range), the only room without a fireplace or a tub big enough for two, is equipped with a queen-sized, half-canopied brass bed. This is the inn's least expensive room.

The rooms in the original cottage are wonderful, but we were most impressed with the more contemporary hideaways in the annex that offer a bit more privacy.

The most expensive of these (mid $200 range) is Renaissance Rose, a bright, two-room suite with a king-sized brass-and-porcelain bed and a tiled fireplace. In the spacious bathroom are a clawfoot tub and shower, both of which should accommodate two.

In the low $200 range is Briar Rose, a second-floor room with a window seat, a queen-sized brass-and-porcelain bed, a fireplace, and a bathroom with a clawfoot tub and a shower for two.

Among the most romantic features of the inn is a large garden gazebo that holds a bubbling spa available to guests by reservation.

The Zaballa House

324 Main Street
Half Moon Bay, CA 94019
Telephone: (415) 726-9123

Nine rooms, each with private bath; four with gas
fireplaces; three with spa tubs for two. Complimentary
full breakfast served at communal table. No handicapped access. Smoking is not permitted. Moderate
to expensive.

Getting There
From Highway 1 in Half Moon Bay, drive east on
Highway 92 to Main Street and turn right. Follow
Main Street to inn on right. Half Moon Bay is approximately twenty-six miles south of San Francisco,
thirty-nine miles from San Jose, and one-hundred-ten
miles from Sacramento.

The Zaballa House

Half Moon Bay

*H*alf Moon Bay's oldest residence, once home to a prominent nineteenth-century family, has recently been putting smiles on the faces of traveling romantics since its rechristening as a charming inn. However, not everything that goes bump in the night here is romantically inspired.

Not long after the owners began renovating the old house and removed an original staircase to create Room 6 upstairs, strange things began happening, but only in Room 6. First there was the guest who in the middle of the night became locked inside the room and awakened the entire house with pounding and yelling. Later there was a flood in the bathroom. Then guests began documenting ghost sightings in the room's diary. During our inspection, the door to Room 6 mysteriously slammed shut.

Rooms for Romance

Despite occasional reports of a spiritual visitor, or possibly because of them, Room 6 (low to mid $100 range) packs 'em in. It's a large room with a handsome four-poster bed, gas fireplace, and a bathroom with a small clawfoot tub.

Our favorite is Room 7 (mid $100 range), with a queen-sized brass bed, a tiled gas fireplace, and a view of Main Street. The big bathroom holds a spa tub for two and a cushy chair. You'll understand why it's called the Rooster Room when you're awakened at sunrise by the cock-a-doodle-dooing from across the street.

The rear-facing Room 9 (low $100 range) is the inn's brightest accommodation. A queen-sized bed sits under the sloping ceiling, and the bathroom has a clawfoot tub.

On the ground floor, our first choice is Room 4 (mid $100 range), with a tiny wicker love seat and a gas fireplace. In the bathroom, a spa tub for two with a shower attachment sits under two windows.

We found Room 5 to be better suited for families than for a romantic getaway. In Room 3, a clawfoot tub and sink are situated in the bedroom. Room 8 has a double bed.

Although The Zaballa House has no yard or garden of its own, guests are invited to stroll the grounds of Flora Farm Nursery next door.

Old Thyme Inn

779 Main Street
Half Moon Bay, CA 94019
Telephone: (415) 726-1616

Seven rooms, each with private bath; four with fireplaces and/or spa tubs for two. Complimentary full
breakfast served at communal table; breakfast is
delivered to guests in the Garden Suite and Thyme
Room. Complimentary wine and refreshments available each evening. No handicapped access. Smoking
is not permitted. Moderate to deluxe.

Getting There

From San Francisco, take Interstate 280 south or
Highway 101 south to Highway 92 west and follow
to Half Moon Bay. Turn left (south) at the first traffic light (Main Street) and drive seven blocks to inn
on left. From Highway 1 in Half Moon Bay, drive
east on Highway 92 to Main Street and turn right.
Follow Main Street for six blocks to inn on left. Half
Moon Bay is approximately twenty-six miles south
of San Francisco, thirty-nine miles from San Jose,
and one-hundred-ten miles from Sacramento.

Old Thyme Inn

Half Moon Bay

*P*arsley, sage, rosemary, and thyme—these and more than sixty other herb varieties
grow in a fragrant garden that serves as the centerpiece of the Old Thyme Inn, a cozy
hundred-year-old Victorian that occupies a Main Street address a few blocks away from the
Half Moon Bay's historic downtown.

George and Marcia Dempsey, who bought the inn in 1992, left respective full-time careers
in law and advertising to host traveling romantics in one of the region's most well-known bed-
and-breakfast inns.

Rooms for Romance

The best room in the house is the Garden Suite (low $200 range), a second-floor hideaway
accessed via a private outdoor stairway off the garden. A queen-sized, canopied, four-poster
bed sits at an angle on rose-colored carpet and a gas fireplace flickers nearby. In one corner of
the room, a skylight illuminates a spa tub for two. This is the only room with an entertainment
center (television, videocassette player, and stereo cassette player). There's also a small refrigerator stocked with complimentary refreshments.

We were also attracted to the Thyme Room (mid $100 range) and the Rosemary Room
(low $100 range) on the first floor. Thyme, a large master bedroom–sized room situated near
the entrance to the inn, has a queen-sized canopied bed, a romantic tub for two, and a fireplace.
Rosemary is a brightly lit room with a stained-glass window and features a bathroom with a
spa tub set under a window near the herb garden.

There are four homespun rooms on the second floor. The Mint Room (mid $100 range)
offers a queen-sized bed, a fireplace, an old-fashioned clawfoot tub, and a peek of the ocean.

Chamomile (around $100), decorated in yellow tones, has a clawfoot tub in an alcove sepa-
rated from the bedroom by lace curtains.

Guests staying in Lavender must leave the room to reach their private bathroom. Oregano,
a sunny corner room, is equipped with an antique French double bed.

SEAL COVE INN

221 Cypress Avenue
Moss Beach, CA 94038
Telephone: (415) 728-7325

Ten rooms, each with private bath, fireplace, telephone, and television with videocassette player; two
with tubs for two. Amenities include a video library,
complimentary soft drinks and wine, evening
refreshments, fresh flowers, and daily newspaper.
Complimentary full breakfast served communally in
dining room or continental breakfast served in your
room. Handicapped access. Smoking is not permitted. Two-night minimum stay required during holiday periods. Expensive to deluxe.

Getting There
From freeways 280 or 101, take Highway 92 exit in
San Mateo west toward Half Moon Bay. At Highway
1 turn north and drive six miles to Moss Beach. Turn
left on Cypress Avenue (at the Moss Beach Distillery
sign) to inn on right. Moss Beach is approximately
twenty miles from San Francisco, fifty miles from
San Jose, and one-hundred miles from Sacramento.

Seal Cove Inn

Moss Beach

*A*fter visiting some fifteen thousand inns around the world, guidebook author Karen Brown decided to see what it was like on the other side of the guest book. So in 1991, she and husband Rick Herbert created, from the ground up, Seal Cove Inn, one of the Bay Area's most romantic retreats.

During her extensive European and domestic travels, Karen has seen the good, the bad, and the ugly, and the couple left nothing to chance when it came time to build their own place. They chose a pretty piece of property near the ocean and designed a striking two-story manor with a steep roof and charming dormers.

Guest rooms are spacious, bathrooms are attractive and contemporary, and each room has a woodburning fireplace and either a balcony or a patio accessed via sliding French doors. Grandfather clocks are an additional nice touch to each room. The Herberts also provide attentive service while respecting the hints of visiting couples who prefer privacy.

Rooms for Romance

Unlike some inns where only the most expensive rooms offer romantic promise, each of Seal Cove Inn's accommodations is fit for a memorable weekend for two.

Provence is one of four downstairs rooms, all of which are offered in the mid $100 range. This retreat has a sofa and a queen-sized bed, as well as an antique rocker.

Our home for a night was Rote Rose (upper $100 range) on the second floor, with a high, queen-sized Jenny Lind bed. Two cushy chairs faced each other between the bed and corner fireplace.

Another seductive second-floor room is Cypress (mid $200 range), with waxed pine furnishings and a hand-made, king-sized Amish tavern bed. A spa tub for two sits under the dormer window in the bathroom.

The inn's largest room is the Fitzgerald (mid $200 range), whose centerpiece is a king-sized canopied bed draped with rich fabric. Nearby is a matching sofa set before the fireplace. Juliette balconies provide a pretty view toward the ocean. In the bathroom is a spa tub for two.

The sea is just a short stroll away, and all guest rooms at Seal Cove Inn have park views with glimpses of the ocean through a distant grove of cypress trees.

The Inn San Francisco

943 South Van Ness Avenue
San Francisco, CA 94110
Telephone: (415) 641-0188 or
toll-free: (800) 359-0913

Twenty-two rooms, seventeen with private baths;
four with fireplaces and tubs for two. Amenities
include terry robes, refrigerators, fresh flowers, and
chocolates. Some garage parking stalls available at
extra charge. Complimentary full breakfast buffet
taken at tables for two or to your bedroom. Hot tub.
No handicapped access. Smoking is allowed. Two-
night minimum stay required during weekends and
holidays periods. Moderate to expensive.

Getting There
From the Golden Gate Bridge, exit at Lombard
Street and drive to Van Ness Avenue. Turn right on
Van Ness, follow past Market Street and turn right
onto South Van Ness to inn. From the Bay Bridge,
follow signs to Highway 101 north/Golden Gate
Bridge. Exit on Mission Street to the right and drive
to South Van Ness Avenue. Turn right on South Van
Ness to inn between Twentieth and Twenty-First
streets.

The Inn San Francisco

San Francisco

*O*ne of San Francisco's original Victorians, this grand Italianate occupies a spot in an ethnically diverse, blue-collar neighborhood in the Mission District on what is known as Mansion Row, a collection of houses that barely escaped the fires following the 1906 earthquake.

In contrast to the neighborhood bustle, the inn is quiet and peaceful inside. Steep stairs lead from the street to the entry and ornate double parlors. More stairs lead to the second and third floors, and a narrow, almost vertical staircase spirals to a breezy rooftop sundeck that overlooks the city.

Rooms for Romance

Rooms classified as "cozy" are priced at around $100 or less. Some of these share bathrooms and have double beds. We don't recommend these for romantic getaways. Those in the "spacious" category have queen-sized feather beds and private baths, and carry rates in the lower $100 range. Deluxe rooms, like those described below, have tariffs in the mid to upper $100 range, and are equipped with spas, hot tubs, and/or fireplaces.

As is often the case in older San Francisco homes, many rooms whose windows are shaded by adjacent buildings are somewhat dark and tend to feature creative uses of space. In some rooms, it appears that bathrooms were once closets and closets used to be crawl spaces. It's fun to sit back and imagine the history behind the sturdy manse.

Room 24 is a third-floor hideaway that overlooks the inn's garden. The room is decorated with dark woods and deep-colored rugs, and holds a queen-sized feather bed quilted in Navy blue. A velveteen couch is set beside a fireplace screen (no fireplace, however). The bathtub area, separated from the actual bathroom, is awash in sunlight and features a deep whirlpool tub for two.

Room 21 is a vision of red, with rich Oriental rugs and a fluffy, queen-sized feather bed dressed in a crimson spread. An antique chaise longue sits by a lace-curtained bay window overlooking South Van Ness Avenue. The room also has a working fireplace, complete with statues and carved tile, and a shower with a tiny square bathtub.

The Garden Cottage Suite (upper $100 range) has a queen-sized bed, separate sitting room, and a private bath.

A partially private garden gazebo holds a communal hot tub that's available twenty-four hours a day.

Mandarin Oriental

222 Sansome Street
San Francisco, CA 94104
Telephone: (415) 885-0999

One-hundred-fifty-eight rooms, each with private
bath and deep soaking tub. Amenities include refrigerators, daily newspaper, robes, and silk slippers.
Silks restaurant and Mandarin Lounge. Handicapped
access. Smoking is allowed. No minimum night stay
required. Deluxe.

Getting There
From the Bay Bridge, exit at Fremont Street and
continue across Market Street to Front Street
(Fremont Street becomes Front Street). Turn left on
Pine Street and right on Sansome Street. From the
San Francisco Airport, follow Highway 101 north
and exit at Fourth and Bryant streets. Turn left on
Third street, cross Market Street (which becomes
Kearny Street), and drive three blocks to Bush Street.
Turn right on Bush Street and left on Sansome Street.

Mandarin Oriental

San Francisco

*T*he Mandarin Oriental is proof that romance doesn't exclusively go hand-in-hand with small cozy country inns. One of our largest recommended Northern California destinations, this lavish one-hundred-fifty-eight-room hotel offers what must rank as one of the most romantic experiences in all the world.

The hotel occupies the top eleven floors of the forty-eight-story, twin California Center towers, connected by glass-enclosed skybridges on the guest-room floors. Guests here are treated to dizzying views of San Francisco along with luxury appointments.

Rooms for Romance

All rooms boast breathtaking city views, and each is furnished with three telephones, a sitting area, and a marble bathroom with deep soaking tub. Some tubs are large enough for two. Rates start in the mid $200 range for what is described as a superior room with a queen-sized bed. Deluxe rooms with king-sized beds are available in the high $200 range.

The premier romantic retreats are the Mandarin Rooms—there are twenty-two of these— where spacious, windowed bathrooms feature panoramic city and bay views from the tub. Our forty-fourth-floor Mandarin room offered a bridge-to-bridge vista that included Coit Tower, the Transamerica Pyramid, Alcatraz, and the financial district. The shimmering view, pictured at the beginning of this regional listing, was especially enchanting at night from the bed and from the luxurious bathroom. As you might expect, such bliss carries a price—about $400 a

night. However, this is an experience you'll not soon forget.

At the time of our visit, the hotel was offering weekend rates that were around $100 less than those noted above. Be sure to ask about special rates for Friday, Saturday, or Sunday stays.

The Mansion at Lakewood

1056 Hacienda Drive
Walnut Creek, CA 94598
Telephone: (510) 945-3600 or
toll free: (800) 477-7898

Seven rooms, each with private bath; two with fireplaces and four with tubs for two. Amenities include
robes, radios and cassette players, and fresh flowers.
Complimentary continental breakfast served at
communal table or in your room. Complimentary
refreshments served every afternoon. Handicapped
access. Smoking is allowed only on outdoor terraces.
No minimum night stay requirement. Moderate to
deluxe.

Getting There
From Highway 680 north of Danville, exit at
Ygnacio Valley Road and turn right. (From Highway
680 south of Concord, exit left at Main Street and
turn left on Ygnacio Valley Road.) Drive one-quarter mile to Homestead Avenue and turn right. Turn
left on Hacienda to inn on left. Announce your
arrival at the gate call box.

The Mansion at Lakewood

Walnut Creek

We were surprised at how quickly the bustle of Walnut Creek transitioned to the country setting occupied by The Mansion at Lakewood, an 1860s-vintage Victorian commanding three wooded acres. This historic country estate is only about three minutes from downtown.

Situated behind white iron gates and trimmed by spacious lawns, this is an elegant getaway destination that should have special appeal to Bay Area couples who would rather spend more time being there than getting there.

Rooms for Romance

Definitely the best room in the house, the Estate Suite (mid $300 range) is one of the north state's most sensuous retreats; there's nothing lacking here. You'll find a king-sized, canopied brass bed raised so high that you'll need steps, and a white woodburning stove. French doors open to a private terrace that overlooks the gardens and gazebo. In the marble bathroom, a whirlpool tub for two sits beneath a window; there's also a giant-sized black shower, two pedestal sinks, and a spacious makeup counter.

The Terrace Suite (low $200 range), the only other room with a fireplace, has a king-sized feather bed, a sitting area, and a bay window offering a view of the front terrace and gardens.

A porcelain tile double shower is the romantic centerpiece of the English-style Country Manor room (mid $100 range), furnished with a four-poster canopied bed. Juliet's Balcony, situated above the Estate Suite, features a balcony overlooking the gardens, a queen-sized feather bed, and a clawfoot tub. The least expensive room is the Attic Hideaway (low $100 range).

The manor's romantic grounds include a gazebo, Adirondack chairs, and a koi pond with a trickling waterfall.

Pelican Inn

10 Pacific Way
Muir Beach, CA 94965
Telephone: (415) 383-6000

Seven rooms, each with private bath. Complimentary full English breakfast served at tables for two in the restaurant or in your room. Restaurant and lounge. No handicapped access in guest rooms. Smoking is allowed in guest rooms; no smoking in dining areas. No minimum night stay required. Moderate to expensive.

Getting There
From Highway 101 north of Sausalito, take the Highway 1/Stinson Beach exit. At the junction (gas station) turn left toward Stinson Beach. Turn left at Muir Woods sign and continue on Highway 1 for two-and-a-half miles to the inn.

Pelican Inn

Muir Beach

A romantic slice of sixteenth-century England, Pelican Inn is a Tudor-style farmhouse that's true to its heritage. Low doorjams, leaded glass windows, English antiques, exposed wooden beams, and full- and half-canopied beds are found throughout the inn. Guest rooms occupy the second floor; a cozy restaurant and pub are located on the ground floor.

The charming half-timbered building enjoys a wooded setting between the ocean and red-woods and is well positioned for a weekend of poking around Marin County's romantic coastal areas. Stinson and Muir beaches are nearby.

Rooms for Romance

Rooms 1 and 7 (mid $100 range) are the largest in the inn. These hold couches while the others have chairs. Room 7 sits under the eaves and has a dormer window.

Little Room 2 (mid $100 range), oft requested and referred to as the "cute room," features a bed that's tucked beneath a cozy, timbered canopy frame.

Rooms 3, 4, and 5 have balconies and overlook the parking area and the woods. Rooms 1, 2, 6, and 7 overlook the lawn, hills, and fields with horses. All rooms have queen-sized beds.

Bathrooms, while not lavish in space or amenities, are functional, just like those of olde England. All have tiled showers except Room 7, which has a bathtub.

Mountain Home Inn

810 Panoramic Highway
Mill Valley, CA 94941
Telephone: (415) 381-9000

Ten rooms, each with private bath; three with fire-places. Complimentary full breakfast served at tables for two or in your room. Restaurant and lounge. No handicapped access. Smoking is allowed in half of the rooms. No minimum night stay required. Moderate to expensive.

Getting There
From the Golden Gate Bridge, exit Highway 101 at Stinson Beach/Highway 1 in Mill Valley. Drive about two-thirds-of-a-mile and turn left at the stop-light onto Highway 1. Follow for two-and-a-half miles. At the Panoramic Highway (the sign says Mt. Tamalpais), turn right and drive for nearly one mile. At the four-way intersection, take the high road, Panoramic. Drive for two miles to inn on right.

Mountain Home Inn

Mill Valley

*T*he often puzzled responses elicited by our mention of the Mountain Home Inn confirm that there are still a few secret places left in the San Francisco Bay area.

Only about a half-hour's drive from downtown San Francisco, this Marin County hideaway commands a lush setting on the lower reaches of 2,600-foot-high Mount Tamalpais. The terraced guest room buildings afford gorgeous views of San Francisco Bay, the Tiburon Peninsula, and Mount Diablo. San Francisco's beloved newspaper columnist, Herb Caen, described the inn as a miniature version of Yosemite's grand Ahwahnee Hotel.

Rooms for Romance

Rooms 1 and 5, called deluxe rooms (lower $200 range), are the most romantic and the most expensive. Both have fireplaces and king-sized beds. Room 1 has a skylight. The bathrooms in these rooms, equipped with spa tubs, open through shutters to the bedrooms and the beautiful views beyond.

Room 6, a similarly equipped retreat located on a lower level facing the redwoods (it also has a nice view), is available for about $20 less. Room 10, which has a bay window and spa tub for two but no fireplace, commands a rate in the mid $100 range.

Standard rooms, furnished with queen-sized beds, are offered in the mid $100 range. Some have private terraces.

If there's no room at the inn during your visit to Marin County, you can always drop by for a romantic meal on the deck overlooking the north Bay Area or at a dining room table next to a fireplace. And don't overlook the romantic vistas from atop Mount Tam just a short drive from the inn.

TEN INVERNESS WAY BED AND BREAKFAST

10 Inverness Way
Inverness, CA 94937
Telephone: (415) 669-1648

Five rooms, each with private bath. Complimentary full breakfast served at communal tables. Breakfast delivered to guests in Room 3. Spa. No handicapped access. Smoking is not permitted. Two-night minimum stay required during weekends; three-night minimum during holiday periods. Moderate.

Getting There
From Highway 101 north of San Francisco, take the San Anselmo/Sir Francis Drake Boulevard exit, and follow Sir Francis Drake for about forty-five minutes to Highway 1. Turn right on Highway 1 and left on Bear Valley Road. Drive about three miles to stop sign and turn left, following road for four miles to Inverness. Turn left at the second Inverness Way sign. Inn is on the right.

Ten Inverness Way Bed and Breakfast

Inverness

*U*nlike many innkeepers who provide visitors with pages of things to do in the area, Mary Davies offers her guests a list of great books to read. Ten Inverness Way is a book lover's dream, a quiet, cozy retreat, perfect for cuddling, relaxing, and for diving into that novel that you've not had time to open.

Just the sight of this shingled charmer, surrounded by flowers, plants, and trees, drove the stress from our road-weary bodies. A walk up the stairs to the homey second-level living area made us want to slink into a couch and melt away.

Rooms for Romance

Situated on the lower level just off the entry, Room 3 (mid $100 range) is the inn's most spacious and the most private. Inside are a love seat, a small table and chairs, and a tiny kitchen. The bathroom has a tub and shower combination. French doors open onto a private gravel garden patio. Breakfast is delivered to guests staying in this room, if requested.

Room 4 is a nicely lit corner that faces the rear and side of the property. Room 5 offers a view of trees from the bed. Tomales Bay is partially visible from Room 2, a front-facing room whose bathroom is placed under a skylit eave. These rooms, whose bathrooms are equipped with showers, are offered in the lower $100 range.

Because the rooms here are quite small (most are furnished with but one cushy chair in addition to a queen-sized bed), guests tend to congregate in the inn's comfortable living room, which contains a stone fireplace, sofas, and chairs, in addition to a guitar and a player piano. Couples may also reserve time in the very private hot tub room at the rear of the property, accessed by a garden path.

The Monterey Bay Area

DAYTIME DIVERSIONS

Tor House, the enchanting stone farmhouse of poet Robinson Jeffers, is open for tours Fridays and Saturdays. You'll find it at 26304 Ocean View Avenue near Stewart Way in Carmel. Just inside the lower gate of Carmel Mission, follow Mission Trail to a meadow with a couple of benches. Be sure to take time out from shopping for a stroll along the white sandy beach in Carmel.

At the foot of Forest Avenue in Pacific Grove is popular Lovers Point Park, which offers a sandy cove and beautiful vistas. A spectacular bayside bike/walking path connects Pacific Grove with Monterey via Cannery Row.

Santa Cruz visitors will enjoy a bicycle ride on an equally impressive pedestrian/bike trail that winds along West Cliff Drive between the wharf and Natural Bridges State Park.

TABLES FOR TWO

In Carmel, our innkeepers gave the most stars to Sans Souci (Lincoln Avenue between Fourth and Fifth avenues), Anton and Michel (Mission Street at Seventh Avenue), and La Boheme on the corner of Dolores Street and Seventh Avenue.

In Pacific Grove, The Centrella (see listing in this section) is within walking distance of the Old Bath House (620 Ocean View Boulevard), a restaurant that overlooks the bay.

The Shadowbrook, a restaurant in Capitola (1750 Wharf Road), is one of Northern California's most romantic dining spots. A funicular transports diners down a steep wooded hillside to the restaurant nestled beside the quiet Soquel River.

AFTER HOURS

Decadent desserts and drinks are served on a heated outdoor terrace at La Playa Hotel in Carmel (see listing in this section). The Bay Club is a restaurant in the Inn at Spanish Bay (on the Seventeen Mile Drive in Pebble Beach) that typically offers mellow music and desserts and drinks until around 10:00 p.m.

The beachside coffee shops and restaurants of Capitola attract local and visiting couples after hours, especially during weekends. While Santa Cruz's downtown Pacific Garden Mall is worth a daytime visit, we don't recommend walking here after dark.

Babbling Brook Inn

1025 Laurel Street
Santa Cruz, CA 95060
Telephone: (408) 427-2437 or
toll-free: (800) 866-1131

Twelve rooms, each with private bath and television; ten with fireplaces. Complimentary full breakfast buffet taken at tables for two in the lobby area. Complimentary wine and appetizers served each afternoon. Handicapped access. Smoking is not permitted. Two-night minimum stay required for Saturday reservations. Moderate to expensive.

Getting There
From Highway 17 or Highway 1 in Santa Cruz, follow signs to Highway 1 north/Half Moon Bay. (Highway 1 is called Mission Street in Santa Cruz.) Follow Mission Street to Laurel Street and turn left. Follow Laurel Street to inn on right.

Babbling Brook Inn

Santa Cruz

Many inns—some with dramatic ocean views—have opened in the Santa Cruz area in recent years. To many central coast visitors, however, the Babbling Brook Inn, Santa Cruz's first B & B, remains the favorite, despite its location several blocks away from the ocean.

Occupying a lush setting along the banks of a creek from which it draws its name, the Babbling Brook consists of a historic residence housing four rooms and three attractive, two-story brown-shingled buildings. Each room has a view of the brook or the romantic gardens. There's even a quaint little covered bridge and a waterwheel.

However, the Babbling Brook Inn is situated along a somewhat busy residential street, and traffic can be heard from some rooms, especially during the daytime. The beach and the Santa Cruz Municipal Wharf are within walking distance. A bike trail runs for several miles along enchanting West Cliff Drive from the wharf to Natural Bridges State Park.

Rooms for Romance

The Babbling Brook tempts visitors with a delectable variety of country French–style accommodations. This isn't your typical, four- or five-room B & B. It'll take you twelve visits to sample all the rooms here.

The Pissarro (around $100) features a hexagonal window area that looks over the brook and a private garden-level deck accessed through French doors. There's also a deep soaking tub that, alas, is only big enough for one.

The half-timbered walls and Laura Ashley decor of the Honeymoon Suite (low to mid $100 range) convey a decidedly English feel. This room contains a king-sized, canopied four-poster bed and a raised corner woodburning stove, and it has a private balcony overlooking the huge waterwheel. In the bathroom is an unusual, romantic European-style antique tub (it's big enough for two) recessed in wood. Guests in this room are treated to breakfast in bed.

Centerpiece of the Degas Room (low $100 range) is an impressive ten-foot-tall, white wrought-iron bed created for a production of Romeo and Juliet at the University of California, Santa Cruz. This cozy room sits right above the brook.

In the FMRS Garden Room (low $100 range), a large window overlooks the garden. This room is equipped with a woodburning stove and a king-sized bed, and the bathroom here is the inn's largest.

Monet (mid $100 range), a second-floor room overlooking the garden and brook, has a bathroom with a tiled tub for two set under a pentagonal window and a skylight. The room has a draped and canopied bed, a woodburning stove, and a small balcony.

The Inn at Depot Hill

250 Monterey Avenue
Capitola, CA 95010
Telephone: (408) 462-3376 or
toll-free: (800) 572-2632

Eight rooms, each with private bath, private entry, woodburning fireplace, tub or shower for two, robes, television with videocassette player, and cassette stereo system. Complimentary full breakfast served at communal table, tables for two, or in your room. Handicapped access. Smoking is permitted on private patios only. Two-night minimum required if staying on a Saturday night; two-night minimum during holiday periods. Expensive to deluxe.

Getting There
From Highway 1 south of Santa Cruz, take the Park Avenue exit west toward the bay. After one mile, turn left on Monterey Avenue and make an immediate left into the inn's parking lot.

The Inn at Depot Hill

Capitola

*T*hank your lucky stars for the demise of the train that once shuttled San Francisco passengers to the beach community of Capitola. Had the old "Suntan Special" not given way to the automobile, The Inn at Depot Hill might still be a cold and drab railway station.

The 1901-vintage depot had been serving as a private residence when owner Suzie Lankes and partner Dan Floyd arrived on the scene a few years ago. It took ten months of new construction and renovation to create what we believe is the central coast's most luxurious inn.

Early on, Lankes considered modeling the guest rooms after the opulent Orient Express, but she ultimately headed in a different direction, instilling them with the essence of various destinations that might once have been served by vintage trains. These days your ticket will take you to such storied locales as Portofino and Paris.

Rooms for Romance

The Paris Room (around $200), which opens onto the inn's main garden, is specially designed for a lusty getaway. A fireplace separates the living room and bedroom, whose windows are covered with French lace. Soft lighting from Louis XVI lamps completes the mood. In the black-and-white marbled bathroom is a spacious shower with a spigot for each of you.

The inn's least expensive room, Stratford-on-Avon (mid $100 range), is a sunny retreat reminiscent of an English cottage. This pretty room offers a long window seat with cushy pillows and a bathroom with a two-person marble shower. The domed ceiling over the bed is illuminated with ultra-romantic adjustable lighting.

In addition to a handsome draped bed and love seat, the English garden–style Sissinghurst Room (high $100 range) features a private patio with its own outdoor spa. There's also a shower for two in the bathroom.

The Portofino, Sissinghurst, Delft, and Cote d'Azur rooms have their own patios as well as outdoor spas tucked into gazebo-type enclosures for privacy.

Those for whom a visit to a former depot wouldn't be complete without a night aboard a train will not be disappointed with the sumptuous Railroad Baron's Room (low $200 range), bedecked with rich trappings like those enjoyed in the private Pullman cars of yesteryear. Warm dark woods, gold leafing, upholstered walls, and tassled draperies are combined with a fancy bathroom with a deep tub for two. Even if you don't sleep in this spectacular room, ask to see it if it's vacant. All aboard!

Hotel Pacific

300 Pacific Street
Monterey, CA 93940
Telephone: (408) 373-5700 or
toll-free: (800) 554-5542

One-hundred-five rooms, each with private bath, fireplace, two televisions, and three telephones. Amenities include terry robes, refrigerators, underground parking, room service, and concierge service. Complimentary continental breakfast served communally; can be delivered to your room for a small charge. Courtyard spas and restaurant. Handicapped access. Smoking is allowed. Two-night minimum stay required during weekends and holiday periods. Expensive to deluxe.

Getting There
From Highway 1, take the Soledad exit in Monterey and proceed through the stop light. Turn right on Pacific Street and follow to inn downtown.

Hotel Pacific

Monterey

*A*mong the newest of our recommended coastal destinations, Hotel Pacific is a great place to stay for those who delight in the sights, smells, and sounds of the coast and who enjoy the contemporary conveniences—like underground parking and room service—that a newer hotel has to offer.

In Monterey's historically rich downtown peppered with graceful Spanish-style buildings, Hotel Pacific blends nicely with a colorfully landscaped adobe-style façade. Cars are tucked conveniently out of sight in a parking garage below the guest rooms. It appears much smaller than its one-hundred-five-room size would indicate.

The hotel is a collection of more than a dozen tiered structures built around three courtyards. They're connected by a maze of pathways made of terra cotta tiles, and the grounds are lush with plants and flowers.

Rooms for Romance

Wood, plaster, and tile figure prominently in the guest rooms, some of which have bay views. The goosedown feather beds are posted with peeled logs, and hardwood floors are covered with hand-woven rugs. All rooms have fireplaces and private patios or balconies and are equipped with two televisions (one is in the bathroom) and three telephones. Tubs and separate showers are found in each bathroom.

Suite 426 (mid $200 range), our home for a night, was an ocean-view end unit in which the draped king-sized bed was separated from a small living area by a tiled counter. The love seat facing a fireplace invited cuddling, and a small balcony beckoned with a bay view. The sound of the courtyard fountain below enhanced an already romantic atmosphere. Rooms without views start in the mid $100 range.

Hotel Pacific is within walking distance of Fisherman's Wharf, historic sites, and the Monterey-to-Pacific Grove pedestrian/bicycle path that runs through Cannery Row. Also a short stroll away are the peninsula's longest stretch of beach and the popular Monterey Bay Aquarium.

At the time of our visit, the hotel was offering various specially priced getaway packages available Sunday through Thursday.

The Centrella

612 Central Avenue
Pacific Grove, CA 93950
Telephone: (408) 372-3372 or
toll free: (800) 233-3372

Twenty-six rooms, all but two with private baths;
five rooms with fireplaces. Complimentary full
breakfast buffet; seating at communal tables and
tables for two. Complimentary wine and appetizers
served every afternoon. Handicapped access.
Smoking is not permitted. Two-night minimum
stay on weekends from June through September
and during holiday periods. Moderate to expensive.

Getting There
From southbound Highway 1, take Pebble Beach/
Pacific Grove exit (Highway 68 west) and follow
signs to Pacific Grove. Continue on Forest Avenue
into downtown Pacific Grove, cross Lighthouse
Avenue, and drive one block to Central Avenue. Turn
left on Central Avenue and drive two blocks to inn.

The Centrella

Pacific Grove

*I*t seems like yesterday that we watched workers transform an ugly duckling into a graceful swan. When we first happened by the decrepit, hundred-year-old boarding house in the early 1980s, it appeared as though the building was being torn down. Actually, owners Dr. Joe Megna and Gary Jones left the weathered but elegant façade intact and completely gutted the interior. In the process they created The Centrella, an upscale inn with a handsome vintage appearance.

Occupying a sunny corner in a residential area, the blue-and-white inn is a short walk from the bay as well as from quaint downtown shops and restaurants. Few rooms have bay views, however.

Breakfast and late afternoon refreshments are laid out in a spacious parlor/dining room. Guests may sit at tables of six or eight or at small tables for two against windows that face a side yard area.

Rooms for Romance

There are seven rooms on the first floor, but for romantic reasons we prefer the top two floors of the main building and the four adjacent cottage units.

The top floor is given to two spacious suites with dormer windows, each offered in the mid $100 range. In the Vera Franklin Suite, a pretty, queen-sized brass-and-iron bed is illuminated by two skylights. A sitting area with a settee and cushy chair is situated under the eaves. The dormer window offers a peek of Monterey Bay.

The adjacent Anna Bieghle Suite has skylights, a king-sized bed, and a sitting area with a love seat and wet bar. The bathrooms of both suites have pedestal sinks and clawfoot tubs.

Our favorite on the second floor is Room 22 (low to mid $100 range), a nicely windowed corner with matching floral-print wallpaper and draperies. The king-sized brass-and-iron bed, dressed in pretty white linens, is flanked by antique tables with small stained-glass lamps. There's a clawfoot tub in the bathroom.

Just off the inn's rose garden sits the storybook-style R. L. Holman Suite (upper $100 range), decorated in coral and heather-green tones. This spacious retreat has a bay window with a table and two chairs and a living room with a wet bar, a television, and a sofa facing a fireplace. In the bedroom is a queen-sized iron bed.

The John Steinbeck Suite (upper $100 range) is a second-story cottage unit that includes a living room with a fireplace and a sofa and a separate bedroom with a king-sized bed.

Furnishings at The Centrella are a comfortable mix of antique beds and dressers, chairs, and sofas with contemporary fabrics, and wicker.

Gatehouse Inn Bed and Breakfast

225 Central Avenue
Pacific Grove, CA 93950
Telephone: (408) 649-8436

Nine rooms, each with private bath; six with wood stoves. Complimentary full buffet breakfast served at communal table and tables for two, or can be taken to your room. Complimentary refreshments available round-the-clock. Smoking is not permitted. No minimum stay requirements. Moderate to expensive.

Getting There
From southbound Highway 1, take Pebble Beach/ Pacific Grove exit (Highway 68 west) and follow signs to Pacific Grove. Continue on Forest Avenue and turn right at Central Avenue. Drive seventeen blocks to inn.

Gatehouse Inn Bed and Breakfast

Pacific Grove

We've been combing the streets of this Victorian village for years, but we continue to uncover romantic secrets. Among the most romantic is this charmer situated only about a block from Monterey Bay.

Reportedly admired by novelist John Steinbeck, whose family lived across the street, the Gatehouse was built in 1884 by a California senator as a summer home. In more recent years the interior has been tastefully redone to provide niceties, such as private baths and fireplaces, that traveling couples appreciate.

Unlike some dark and dreary Victorians we've visited, the Gatehouse is a particularly bright, airy, and cheerful structure, especially on those sunny days that paint the Monterey Bay skies a vivid blue. Several rooms have bay views.

Rooms for Romance

The Captain's Room, our personal favorite, is accessed via a separate entrance around the back of the house. This remote hideaway has a private covered porch and looks out over a small side yard to the bay. The private bathroom, whose door has a ship's porthole, has a claw-foot tub.

The bay-view Langford Suite (upper $100 range) is probably the inn's most romantically styled room. Enlarged from two smaller rooms, this sunny corner holds a queen-sized bed partially canopied in lace. Next to the bed is a pretty, white, antique wood stove that shares a tiled hearth with a clawfoot tub. The original wood floors are covered with area rugs.

At the rear of the house on the second floor is the Sun Room (mid $100 range), a smaller room with a queen-sized, white iron bed. The windowed walls afford a view that takes in Monterey Bay, and the bathroom contains a clawfoot tub.

Also worthy of note is the second-floor Doc Ricketts Room (mid $100 range), where an artfully papered ceiling design will entertain you from the queen-sized brass bed. The Doc Ricketts and Cannery Row rooms are the inn's two most unusually decorated accommodations. We weren't particularly impressed with the Otter's Cove or Steinbeck rooms as romantic retreats.

At press time, the Gatehouse Inn was undergoing a change in ownership. Comments from our readers about their impressions are welcome.

La Playa Hotel Cottages

Camino Real at Eighth Avenue (P.O. Box 900)
Carmel, CA 93921
Telephone: (408) 624-6476

Seventy-five rooms and five cottages, each with
private bath. Swimming pool. Restaurant and lounge.
Handicapped access. Smoking is allowed. Two-night
minimum stay required during weekends; three-night
minimum stay required during holiday periods.
Moderate to deluxe.

Getting There
From Highway 1, exit at Ocean Avenue and drive
west into Carmel. Turn left on Camino Real to
Eighth Avenue to hotel.

La Playa Hotel Cottages

Carmel

*W*e've long been impressed with the entire La Playa estate, but from a purely romantic perspective, the five dreamy cottages are our favorites. The cottages, which range in size from one to four bedrooms, are nestled among the pine and cypress trees along a peaceful residential street a block and a half from the main hotel.

Rooms for Romance

The least expensive (low $200 range) is Skyway, a cozy unit with separate living and sleeping areas, as well as an outdoor terrace.

Two larger cottages, Homeport and Moongate (around $300), are similarly laid out. These have king-sized beds in the bedrooms, fireplaces, full kitchens, and outdoor patios.

The other two, Tradewinds and Loghaven, are intended to house multiple couples and families. These accommodate six and eight people, respectively.

While we've focused our attention on the cottages, La Playa's two hotel buildings hold seventy-five very comfy rooms, some of which offer ocean views.

Carriage House Inn

Junipero Street between Seventh and Eighth
Avenues (P.O. Box 1900)
Carmel, CA 93921
Telephone: (408) 625-2585

Thirteen rooms, each with private bath and fireplace;
eight with tubs for two. Complimentary continental
breakfast brought to your room. No handicapped
access. Smoking is allowed in some rooms. Two-
night minimum stay required during weekends and
holiday periods. Expensive to deluxe.

Getting There
From Highway 1, exit at Ocean Avenue and drive
west into Carmel. Turn left on Junipero Street and
drive one-and-a-half blocks to inn on right.

Carriage House Inn

Carmel

We discovered Carriage House Inn during a visit to its charming next door neighbor, the Cobblestone Inn, which is featured in our first Northern California romantic getaway guide. Fairly nondescript from the outside, Carriage House can only be completely appreciated from within, that is if you're lucky enough to book a room. The inn was full during our first visit, and we had to come back another day in order to preview some guest rooms.

Rooms for Romance

We recommend the upstairs rooms, which have vaulted ceilings and either Japanese-style soaking tubs for two (our personal favorites) or spa tubs designed for one person. Rooms 2, 8, 9, 10, 11, and 14 have the Japanese-style tubs. The most often-requested rooms are 12, with a spa tub for one, and 8, with a soaking tub for two.

The ultimate romantic retreat here is the Master Suite, with separate sitting and bedroom areas. The sitting room has a sofabed and the bedroom contains a queen-sized bed. The other rooms have king-sized four-poster beds.

At the time of our visit, all but one of the rooms were being offered in the upper $100 range. The Master Suite carries a rate in the mid $200 range.

All rooms at Carriage House Inn have fireplaces, antiques, an English country decor, and down pillows and comforters. All rooms except three have cozy window seats by the fireplaces. There are no ocean views; rooms look out onto the trees.

TICKLE PINK INN

155 Highland Drive
Carmel, CA 93923
Telephone: (408) 624-1244 or
toll free: (800) 635-4774

Thirty-five rooms, each with private bath; sixteen
with woodburning fireplaces. Amenities include
terry robes, daily newspaper, and televisions with
videocassette players in all rooms. Complimentary
continental breakfast served at tables for two or in
your room. Complimentary wine and appetizers
served every evening. Lounge. No handicapped
access. Smoking is allowed. Two-night minimum
stay required on weekends; three-night minimum
during holiday periods. Expensive to deluxe.

Getting There
From Carmel, drive south on Highway 1 for four
miles. Turn left on Highland Drive and follow to
inn on right.

Tickle Pink Inn

Carmel

Several decades ago, on the site now occupied by this popular romantic destination, Bess and Edward Tickle lived in a stone cottage overlooking the rugged coast. Inspired by the constant display of flowers—primarily pink ones—in the Tickles' garden, someone suggested they name their little hideaway Tickle Pink.

The original Tickle Pink is long gone, but when the Gurries family built this resort hotel on the Tickle property in the early 1950s, they retained the playful name, which, like that of its neighbor, the Highlands Inn, has since become synonymous with coastal romance in Northern California.

The venerable cliffside inn, which underwent much-needed cosmetic surgery around 1990, is now hosting its second generation of traveling romantics, as evidenced by an inscription found in a room diary. "Mom and Dad spent their honeymoon in this very suite twenty-seven years ago," wrote a just-married Chicago couple. "I hope we can come back for every anniversary."

Rooms for Romance

There are three classifications of rooms at Tickle Pink. Cove-view rooms command tariffs in the lower to upper $100 range, but for just a few dollars more you can have an ocean-view room. Ocean-view suites, the inn's prime accommodations, carry rates from the high $100 range to the mid $200 range. Most rooms have private balconies and about half contain woodburning fireplaces.

Room 6, an ocean-view suite decorated in tasteful rose, camel, and cream hues, features a canopied king-sized bed and a love seat and chairs set beside the fireplace. The ocean is visible from the sitting area, bedroom, and deck.

Room 23, one of Tickle Pink's largest suites, is decorated in aqua and blue tones, and is lavishly furnished with a sectional couch, two televisions, a wet bar, and a king-sized bed from which you'll have a grand water view. In the bathroom is a black tile-rimmed whirlpool tub for two.

Guest room decks at Tickle Pink, while offering delectable views, are not completely private, and to ensure complete privacy in your room you'll need to close the drapes.

MISSION RANCH

26270 Dolores Street
Carmel, CA 93923
Telephone: (408) 624-6436

Thirty-one rooms, each with private bath; fifteen
with fireplaces and sixteen with oversized tubs.
Complimentary continental breakfast served in the
ranch's restaurant. Exercise room and tennis courts.
Handicapped access. Smoking is not permitted.
Two-night minimum stay required during weekends;
two- or three-night minimum stay required during
holiday periods. Moderate to deluxe.

Getting There
From Highway 1, turn west on Rio Road. Turn left
on Lasuen Drive (at Carmel Mission) and follow
to inn on left.

Mission Ranch

Carmel

*F*irst he gave us the famous Hog's Breath Inn. Now, actor-director Clint Eastwood tempts couples with another reason to visit Carmel: Mission Ranch.

Originally a working ranch and dairy farm, the property later became one of Carmel's best-known resorts. Eastwood, who purchased the ranch buildings and several gorgeous acres in 1986 while serving as Carmel's mayor, personally supervised its rehabilitation and reopening. He even handpicked the handsome country-style wooden beds you'll be sleeping on.

Rooms for Romance

Accommodations at Mission Ranch are not only romantic, they're among Carmel's best bargains. Rates here start at around $100. Of course, the more romantic your room, the higher the price. The luscious Meadow View Rooms (low $200 range), for example, have picture windows that frame either the distant ocean, Point Lobos, or grazing sheep. These are equipped with king-sized beds, spa tubs, fireplaces, and either patios or decks.

The Hay Loft Bedroom (upper $100 range), housed in an old barn building, contains a king-sized bed, pot belly stove, spa tub, and boasts an ocean view.

Built in 1852, the Bunkhouse is the ranch's oldest structure. Now completely restored, the house (around $200) holds a separate living room, dining room, and bedroom, as well as a kitchen.

The stately farmhouse, which dates from the 1860s, contains six bedrooms (low to mid $100 range) and a cushy parlor.

The Honeymoon Cottage (around $200), restored in 1994, was used as a location in the 1950s movie *A Summer Place*. The sitting room in this romantic retreat has a fireplace.

Mission Ranch also offers a restaurant and a piano bar. The ranch is only one block from Carmel Mission and a half mile from the upscale Barnyard and Crossroads shopping centers.

The Gold Country to Lake Tahoe (Including Sacramento)

DAYTIME DIVERSIONS

In Sacramento, take a romantic (daytime only) stroll through the lush grounds of the state capitol. Mature trees and gardens abound. Touristy Old Sacramento, with its woodplank sidewalks, cobblestone streets, and dozens of specialty shops, is a great place to spend part of an afternoon. You can walk from here to Sacramento's impressive Downtown Plaza shopping mall.

Visitors to Lake Oroville Bed and Breakfast have close access to Bidwell Canyon Marina and its flotilla of rental water craft.

In Murphys, visit the romantic wine caves at Kautz Vineyards, on Six Mile Road, and peaceful Stevenot Winery, a couple of miles out of town near Mercer Cavern off Sheep Ranch Road. Visitors to Moaning Cavern outside Murphys descend a circular staircase into a naturally beautiful subterranean "room" with incredible rock formations. The quaint downtown areas of Grass Valley and Nevada City are chockablock with antique and specialty shops.

In South Lake Tahoe, there's nothing quite like a sunset ride on the aerial tram to the top of Heavenly Valley. Take Ski Run Boulevard from Highway 50 up the mountain to Heavenly Valley. Taking Ski Run Boulevard toward the lake will bring you to the berth of the Tahoe Queen, a paddlewheeler with a glass-bottom viewing area. Another sternwheeler, the M. S. Dixie, plies the emerald lake from Zephyr Cove Marina on Highway 50 on the Nevada side of the lake.

At the top of the tram in Squaw Valley, the two of you can ice skate twelve months a year.

There are bike rentals at Richardson's Resort a couple of miles north of South Lake Tahoe on Highway 89.

TABLES FOR TWO

Within an easy drive of Lake Oroville Bed and Breakfast (see listing in this section) is Lake Madrone restaurant (3 Lakeside Drive) in Berry Creek. Sacramento visitors will enjoy Biba (2801 Capitol Avenue) and Chanterelle at the Sterling Hotel (1300 H Street).

Visitors to Nevada City will enjoy Potiger's at Selaya's (320 Broad Street) and Michael's Menu (315 Broad Street). In remote Sierra City, the restaurant pickings are slim; however, try Carlo's Ristorante at the Busch & Heringlake Country Inn (see listing in this section) or the Sierra Buttes Inn (Highway 49 at Hayes Road).

In South Lake Tahoe, we recommend the Fresh Ketch (Tahoe Keys Marina) and Nephele's (1169 Ski Run Boulevard). The Beacon (Highway 89 at Camp Richardson) is a great place to enjoy your favorite beverage with a magnificent lake view.

Amber House Bed-and-Breakfast Inn

1315 Twenty-Second Street
Sacramento, CA 95816
Telephone: (916) 447-1548

Nine rooms, each with private bath and television; five with spa tubs for two. Most have videocassette players. Complimentary bicycle rental for guests. Complimentary full breakfast served at communal table, tables for two, or in your room. No handicapped access. Smoking is not permitted. Moderate to deluxe.

Getting There
From Interstate 5 in Sacramento, exit at J Street and drive through town to Twenty-Second Street. Turn right and drive three-and-a-half blocks to inn, between Capitol Avenue and N Street. The inn is eight blocks from the state capitol.

Amber House Bed-and-Breakfast Inn

Sacramento

*W*e're the first to admit that California's capital city doesn't roll off the tongue as a logical romantic getaway destination, but we continue to discover sumptuous destinations here that have definite appeal.

Sacramento's charming, tree-shaded midtown area, which has been enjoying a renaissance of late, is the setting for Amber House Bed-and-Breakfast Inn, a two-home compound offering visitors a variety of deluxe romantic accommodations.

Rooms for Romance

Poet's Refuge is a Craftsman-style home with intriguing vintage features such as a boxed-beam ceiling, hardwood floors, and a clinker-brick fireplace. The best room here is Lord Byron (mid $100 range), where an oval Jacuzzi tub presides over a gorgeous bathroom of pink Italian marble.

Longfellow (mid $100 range) also has a romantic bathroom with an antique porcelain tub illuminated by a skylight. Two rooms in the Poet's Refuge have double beds.

Next door is our personal favorite, the Artist's Retreat, a restored, 1913 Mediterranean-style home. Renoir (around $200) is a mini-suite with a king-sized bed and modified canopy. In the marbled bathroom is a Jacuzzi tub for two and separate shower.

Degas has a queen-sized canopied bed and a beautiful bathroom with peach-toned tile, a Jacuzzi tub for two, and a separate shower. Van Gogh features an unusual, ultra-romantic solarium bathroom with glass walls and ceiling. In one corner, on a green-and-white checkerboard marble floor, is a heart-shaped Jacuzzi tub for two.

Dunbar House, 1880

271 Jones Street
Murphys, CA 95247
Telephone: (209) 728-2897

Four rooms, each with private bath, woodburning stove, refrigerator with complimentary bottle of wine, and television with videocassette player; one room with spa tub for two. Complimentary full breakfast served at a communal table, tables for two, or in your room. Complimentary afternoon refreshments. No handicapped access. Smoking is not permitted. Two-night minimum stay required during weekends; three-night minimum stay required during holiday periods. Moderate to expensive.

Getting There
From Highway 4 in Angels Camp, drive eight miles east to Murphys. Turn left on Main Street; then left on Jones, and follow to inn on left. From Murphys Grade Road in Angels Camp, drive eight miles east to Murphys. Turn right on Main Street and drive through town to Jones Street. Turn right on Jones Street to inn on right.

Dunbar House, 1880

Murphys

*I*n our romantic opinion, Murphys is to the Gold Country what Carmel is to the Central Coast. Although it's off the beaten track—and possibly because of it—this charming burg keeps calling us back.

Unlike many Mother Lode towns that have traded their original identities for fast-food joints, trailer parks, and modern industry, Murphys is still squarely grounded in the mid 1800s. On Main Street, old-fashioned raised walkways pass under balconied false-fronted

shops selling wares from antiques to dry goods. Hollywood filmmakers, drawn by the town's authentic western look, are frequent visitors.

While many folks come for a day, we suggest spending at least a night or two to truly savor the atmosphere. And there's no better romantic retreat than Dunbar House, 1880, an Italianate mansion separated from Main Street by mature trees and a pretty field where horses graze.

Rooms for Romance

This elegant home, set at the edge of a fine old neighborhood, holds four guest rooms, each with antique furnishings and a queen-sized bed. The two downstairs accommodations are Cedar and Sequoia. Cedar (mid $100 range) is the largest and most expensive, offering a private sun porch with a day bed, and a spa tub for two. Sequoia (around $100) has a vintage clawfoot tub placed under a window near the woodburning stove in the bedroom.

The original master bedroom is now called Ponderosa (around $100), from which guests can view the horses across the street and the inn's garden area. The bedroom is accented with Battenburg lace, and the bathroom holds a clawfoot tub-and-shower combination.

The spacious Sugar Pine Suite (around $100) has a sitting room and an alcove with a woodburning stove. An ample-size bathroom contains a clawfoot tub and separate shower.

Murphy's Inn

318 Neal Street
Grass Valley, CA 95945
Telephone: (916) 273-6873

Eight rooms, each with private bath; four have fireplaces. Complimentary full breakfast served at tables
for two. Spa. Handicapped access. Smoking is not
permitted. No minimum night stay requirement.
Moderate.

Getting There
From eastbound Interstate 80 in Auburn, turn left at
the Highway 49/Grass Valley/Nevada City exit and
drive approximately twenty miles to Grass Valley.
Take the Highway 174/Colfax exit, turn left on
South Auburn Street, and turn left on Neal Street.
Inn is on the right at the corner of School Street.
Driving time to Grass Valley from Sacramento is
approximately one hour.

Murphy's Inn

Grass Valley

One of Grass Valley's most cherished landmarks, this Victorian beauty has deep romantic roots. Built over a century ago by mining magnate Edward Coleman, the home was given as a wedding present to his betrothed.

Now operating as an inn under the guidance of Tom and Sue Myers, the graceful home, with its grand veranda and formal parlors, still reflects the opulent lifestyle of its gold rush–era builders.

Rooms for Romance

Theodosia's Suite (low $100 range) on the first floor is the largest and plushest room in the main house. A king-sized brass bed draped with lace and covered with a floral comforter provides a vantage point for enjoying both a woodburning marble fireplace and a veranda. Decorated in cream and rose hues, the suite, originally the home's formal dining room, is furnished with antique chairs and mirrors and old-fashioned knick-knacks. The tiled bathroom is small, with a double shower.

Also on the first floor is the Sequoia Room (around $100), extending off the kitchen with a private entry. This cozy step-down room is covered with burgundy carpet and is equipped with a queen-sized bed and a woodburning stove on a stone hearth. The small bathroom has a clawfoot tub-and-shower combination. A marble sink from the old days features separate hot and cold spigots.

Murphy's Inn also includes Donation Day House across the street. Sara's Suite (low to mid $100 range) has a king-sized bed, a separate living room, a fireplace, a kitchen, and a private entry. The other room here is Hanson Suite (low $100 range), which holds a king-sized bed, a sitting room, and a fireplace.

Guests interested in exploring Grass Valley's historic district needn't bother searching for a parking space. The inn is just a short stroll away.

Flume's End Bed-and-Breakfast Inn

317 South Pine Street
Nevada City, CA 95959
Telephone: (916) 265-9665

Six rooms, each with private bath (one room with detached bath). Complimentary full breakfast served at tables for two or four. Complimentary snacks and beverages available day and night. No handicapped access. Smoking is not permitted. Two-night minimum stay required during weekends and holiday periods. Moderate.

Getting There
From eastbound Interstate 80 in Auburn, turn left at the Highway 49/Grass Valley/Nevada City exit and drive approximately twenty miles to the Broad Street exit in Nevada City. Drive through town on Broad Street and turn left on South Pine, across Spring Street, and across the little bridge to inn. Driving time to Nevada City from Sacramento is approximately one hour.

Flume's End Bed-and-Breakfast Inn

Nevada City

One of the Gold Country's most unusual inns, Flume's End draws its name from a flume that brought Sierra water to a quartz mill which originally occupied this site during the mid nineteenth century. The mill is gone but the flume still presides over the property. Picturesque Gold Run Creek, which flows next to the inn, provides guests with soothing sounds, especially during the summer months when windows are open and the patio and decks can be savored.

The multilevel, Victorian-style inn, built next to the flume against the side of a fairly steep canyon, is full of intriguing staircases, passageways, bays, gables, and windows.

After serving as a residence during the mid-to-late nineteenth century, the inn housed a not-

so-discreet brothel for many years; a secret door for hasty getaways still exists. (Ask about the resident "lost harlot" ghost.)

Proprietors Steve Wilson, a one-time high school teacher, and Terrianne Straw, formerly a vocational rehabilitation administrator, are assisted by Terrianne's gentle, golden retriever guide dogs.

Rooms for Romance

The bright, bay-windowed Master Bedroom (low $100 range) holds a queen-sized bed and a spacious bathroom with a spa tub for two, double sinks, and a shower. A private deck overlooks the creek.

The Creekside and Garden rooms (around $100) are reached by a narrow, wrought-iron spiral staircase. Garden, equipped with a double bed, has a spa tub-and-shower combination and a private deck over the creek. Creekside features a queen-sized bed and boasts a private deck with the best waterfall view. These two rooms share a lower-level sitting area with a gas fireplace, a wet bar, and a television.

High up under the eaves is the Penthouse (around $100), which offers a bird's eye view of the main deck and creek. The bathroom here has a clawfoot tub and pedestal sink.

The rustic Cottage (low to mid $100 range) includes a kitchenette, a woodburning stove, a queen-sized four-poster bed, a love seat and chairs, and a bathroom with a tub-and-shower combination. A private secluded deck overlooks trees and waterfalls.

We don't recommend the Stained Glass Room, whose detached bath is situated an inconvenient distance from the room.

Busch & Heringlake Country Inn

Highway 49
Sierra City, CA 96125
Telephone: (916) 862-1501

Four rooms, each with private bath; two rooms
with spa tubs for two. Continental breakfast
served in the inn's restaurant. Handicapped
access. Smoking is not permitted. No minimum
stay requirement. Moderate.

Getting There
From eastbound Interstate 80 in Auburn, turn
left at the Highway 49/Grass Valley/Nevada
City exit and drive approximately twenty miles
to Nevada City. Stay on Highway 49 (which
takes a sharp left after Nevada City) and follow
toward Downieville for approximately sixty
miles to Sierra City and inn on left.

Busch & Heringlake Country Inn

Sierra City

We waited years for some incurable romantic to create a soul-stirring hideaway in this remote little mountain burg. We were just about to give up hope when we received a letter from the Busch & Heringlake Country Inn. Our wait was over.

The most isolated of our romantic north state hideaways, the Busch & Heringlake is a comfortable, three-story brick building whose function over the past century has ranged from Wells Fargo stage stop to general store. Proprietor Carlo Giuffre, a former investment banker, bought the place in the mid-1980s and renovated it by hand, creating four modern guest rooms on the second level and a cafe on the ground floor. The hospitable innkeeper, who lives above the inn, runs a relaxed, laid-back operation. Clocks run a little slower up here in the mountains.

Rooms for Romance

We recommend the Phoenix and Young America rooms for romantic getaways. Phoenix (low $100 range) is a sunny corner room facing the road, and is the only room with a fireplace. It also has a small seating area, a queen-sized bed, and a private bath with a spa tub for two.

A pink whirlpool tub for two and an adjacent open shower occupy one corner of the Young America Room (around $100). This room, which has a view of the lush hillside out back, is furnished with a queen-sized brass bed.

Marguerite's Room, a fairly standard room (less than $100), holds a queen-sized bed and a private bath with a double-spigot shower. The rustically decorated Cornish Cabin Room (less than $100) has a queen-sized bed.

Lake Oroville Bed and Breakfast

240 Sunday Drive
Berry Creek, CA 95916
Telephone: (916) 589-0700

Six rooms, each with private bath and telephone; five with spa tubs. Amenities include a billiard table, cassette players in all rooms, and complimentary drinks and snacks. Televisions and videocassette players are available on request. Complimentary full breakfast served in dining room. Handicapped access. Smoking is not permitted. Moderate.

Getting There
From Highway 70 in Oroville, exit east at Oroville Dam Boulevard (Route 162) and drive 1.7 miles to Olive Highway (Route 162). Turn right and drive 13.5 miles around Lake Oroville. Just after the Foreman Creek State Recreation Area sign, turn left on Bell Ranch Road and drive one-and-a-half miles on the gravel road (becomes Sunday Drive) to inn on right. Oroville is approximately one-hundred-sixty miles from San Francisco and two-hundred miles from San Jose.

Lake Oroville Bed and Breakfast

Berry Creek

*O*ur theory that the best places are sometimes the most difficult to find was validated again with the discovery of this contemporary charmer in rural Butte County. Located about twenty minutes outside Oroville at the end of a mile-and-a-half gravel road, Lake Oroville Bed and Breakfast ranks as one of our most remote romantic destinations.

Commanding incredible water and valley views from a wooded hilltop high above Lake Oroville, the inn was built in 1992 by proprietors Ron and Cheryl Damberger, former Marin County residents. Constructed as an inn—it's not a reconfigured home—Lake Oroville Bed and Breakfast offers solitude and comfort with extremely reasonable rates. At the time of our visit, all rooms were being offered for around $100 or less.

Rooms for Romance

The small but nicely decorated guest rooms face an expansive wraparound covered porch and have views into the woods or out over the lake. Each room can be accessed either from an interior hallway or from the porch. All rooms except one have cozy bathrooms containing oval-shaped spa tubs that, while not huge, should accommodate two.

Our favorite room, Victorian (around $100), has a million-dollar view of Lake Oroville and a good portion of Northern California through the branches of a majestic old oak tree. (You can see Mt. Diablo on a clear day.) A king-sized bed sits on deep salmon-colored carpeting.

The valley view from Rose Petal (around $100) is equally or more impressive, but it isn't completely private since the window also faces the porch near the inn's entrance. Rose Petal is equipped with mahogany furniture and a king-sized bed.

One of the most oft-requested rooms is Monet (under $100), a bright corner with yellow floral wallpaper and a queen-sized bed. Situated next to the cozy communal sunroom, Monet looks out on the oak-studded hillside.

Vine (less than $100) doesn't have a spa tub, but the nice walk-in shower, designed to accommodate wheelchairs, is big enough for both of you.

SORENSEN'S RESORT

14255 Highway 88
Hope Valley, CA 96120
Telephone: (916) 694-2203 or
toll-free: (800) 423-9949

Twenty-nine cabins, all but two with private baths;
seventeen with woodburning stoves or fireplaces.
Complimentary full breakfast served in restaurant to
guests of certain rooms. Restaurant, cross-country
ski center, and wood-fired sauna. Limited handicapped access. Smoking is not permitted. Two-night
minimum stay required during weekends; three- or
four-night minimum stay required during holiday
periods. Moderate to deluxe.

Getting There
From Sacramento/Placerville, follow Highway 50
toward South Lake Tahoe. At Meyers, turn right
on Highway 89, drive eleven miles to the Highway
88/89 junction and turn left on Highway 88. Resort
is one mile on right.

Sorensen's Resort

Hope Valley

When weekend Tahoe-bound traffic begins to snarl along Highway 50 as far back as Meyers, the smart money turns right (at Highway 89) and heads for Hope Valley. And while the rest of the folks are still crawling toward Stateline, the two of you will be warming your toes in a high Sierra cabin at Sorensen's Resort.

Occupying a heavenly spot along the Carson River in beautiful Hope Valley, about a half-hour away from the South Tahoe casino area, the resort consists of an eclectic mix of older and newer cabins nestled among glistening aspen.

Rooms for Romance

Don't expect the Ritz in the 1930s and 1940s-era cabins; be aware that some of these are basic and rustic, and nightly rates start at less than $100.

Others, however, like the log-walled Snowshoe, Sheepherder, and Creekside with loft bedroom and kitchen (low to mid $100 range) were added only a few years ago and feature contemporary decor and seductive features.

Among the romantic favorites is Waterfir (around $100), surrounded by aspens and set next to a creek. Inside is a double brass bed, a full kitchen, and a woodstove with a rock hearth. Rockcreek (mid $100 range) is a two-level cabin with a kitchen, dining room, and living room with a couch, and a sleeping loft with a queen-sized bed.

Two of the resort's most popular cabins were once part of Santa's Village, an old amusement park in Scotts Valley near Santa Cruz. After the park was abandoned, the cabins were taken apart and transported to Sorensen's where they've been transformed into luxury hideaways. One of these, the Chapel (mid $100 range), is an old-fashioned log cabin with white chinking and hand-hewn doorways.

The other, called St. Nick's (mid $100 range), retains the enchanting, carved window shutters and flower boxes of the original. However, the cabin now boasts a spa tub for two, a fireplace, a sunny deck, and a bedroom loft reached by a circular staircase. Mr. and Mrs. Santa never had it this good.

With a seven-thousand-foot elevation that attracts winter skiers, Sorensen's offers summer activities that include hiking, fishing, and bicycling. The resort also sponsors numerous special programs each year related to hobbies, the arts, cooking, and recreation.

The Tahoe Seasons Resort

3901 Saddle Road
South Lake Tahoe, CA 96157
Telephone: (916) 541-6700

One-hundred-seventy rooms, each with private
bath and tub for two; most with fireplaces, videocassette players, refrigerators, and wet bars. Room
service breakfast is available with certain package
deals. Swimming pool, spa, tennis courts, underground parking, cafe, and lounge. Handicapped
access. Smoking is allowed. Moderate to deluxe.

Getting There
From Highway 50 in South Lake Tahoe, take Ski
Run Boulevard (away from the lake), follow to
Needle Peak Road, and turn left. Turn right on
Wildwood Road and left on Saddle Road. From
Sacramento/Placerville via Highway 50, avoid the
often heavy South Tahoe–bound traffic by turning
right on Pioneer Trail just past Meyers and follow-
ing to Keller Road. Turn right on Keller Road and
left on Saddle Road. Resort is on the left.

The Tahoe Seasons Resort

South Lake Tahoe

A cozy little inn on the lake it's not. With one-hundred-seventy rooms, it's the largest of our north state destinations, and from the outside, the multi-storied building is fairly nondescript. What's more, a location across the street from Heavenly Valley affords no views of the lake.

If you're wondering what makes The Tahoe Seasons Resort deserving of a spot among our listing of romantic getaways, step inside one of the spacious suites. The rooms here are some of the most intimate we've found in the Tahoe region.

Rooms for Romance

Constructed more than a decade ago, before romance began to figure into the design of most hotels, inns, and resorts, the Tahoe Seasons was ahead of its time. Accommodations (all are larger than five hundred square feet) consist of one-bedroom suites (low to mid $100 range), each featuring a romantic spa tub for two set between the bedroom and living areas. Hinged privacy screens around the tub open to the living area for a view of the fireplace. A vanity/sink area is adjacent, and the toilet is behind a door.

In addition to queen-sized beds, the suites hold couches, televisions with videocassette players, and small wet bars with microwave ovens. Most have fireplaces. Larger master suites, which can accommodate up to six people, carry rates in the upper $100 range.

Set up much like a hotel, Tahoe Seasons has a large, comfortable lounge area on the first floor, as well as a cafe and bar. Dinner is served during the weekend. Tennis courts are located on the roof, and a swimming pool and spa are also available on site.

THE CHRISTIANIA INN

3819 Saddle Road
South Lake Tahoe, CA 96151
Telephone: (916) 544-7337

Six rooms or suites, each with private bath; four with fireplaces. Complimentary continental breakfast can be delivered to your room. Restaurant and lounge. No handicapped access. Smoking is not permitted. Two-night minimum stay required during weekends and holiday periods. Moderate to expensive.

Getting There
From Highway 50 in South Lake Tahoe, take Ski Run Boulevard (away from the lake), follow to Needle Peak Road, and turn left. Turn right on Wildwood Road and left on Saddle Road. Drive two blocks to inn on left. From Sacramento/Placerville via Highway 50, avoid the often heavy South Tahoe–bound traffic by turning right on Pioneer Trail just past Meyers and following to Wildwood Avenue. Turn right on Wildwood and left on Saddle Road. Inn is on the left.

The Christiania Inn

South Lake Tahoe

*I*n a community characterized by cheesy motels that cater to the casino crowd, the Christiania Inn offers travelers a romantic overnight experience that's unfortunately difficult to duplicate in the Lake Tahoe region.

Known affectionately as the "Chris" by those familiar with its charms, the inn tempts visitors with a half-dozen Swiss country–style rooms set behind a Tyrolean-style façade that faces the slopes of Heavenly Valley. (The ski lifts are within walking distance.)

Rooms for Romance

Three two-story suites (upper $100 range) are the inn's premier romantic accommodations. Suite 4, overlooking Heavenly Valley's famous Gunbarrel run, has a dramatic living area with soaring windows, a woodburning fireplace, and a couch. The loft holds a queen-sized bed under mirrors.

In Suite 5, the lower level has a sitting parlor, a wet bar, a dry sauna, and bathroom. A bedroom with king-sized bed and a living room with a fireplace and a love seat are situated on the upper level.

Suite 6, the other two-story retreat, has a living room with a fireplace on a wood-paneled wall and a king-sized bed. There's also a downstairs living room, a wet bar, and a dry sauna. The bathroom has a one-person spa tub.

Suite 3 (upper $100 range) is decorated in Victorian style and features a wet bar and a living area with a cushy couch set into an arched and windowed nook. A fireplace flickers nearby, and a king-sized bed sits in the adjacent bed chamber.

Room 2, also facing Heavenly Valley, is a small room with a bay-windowed nook holding a tiny table with chairs. Room 1 is the inn's least romantic. At the time of our visit, Rooms 1 and 2 were being offered for less than $100.

The impressive rock fireplaces in the downstairs restaurant and bar create an inviting romantic ambience for after-hours dining and cuddling. When making a dinner reservation, ask for table nine, our romantic favorite, situated next to the fireplace.

Because the inn offers no outdoor living areas, the Christiania is, in our opinion, most ideally suited to winter getaways. However, south shore beaches are just a short drive away. Rates are considerably less in the spring, fall, and winter. The inn does not offer lake views.

Appendix

More Travel Resources for Incurable Romantics

Weekends for Two in Northern California: 50 Romantic Getaways (second edition)
The original romantic travel guide, revised and updated

Weekends for Two in Southern California: 50 Romantic Getaways
Intimate destinations from the Santa Barbara coast to the sultry desert

Weekends for Two in the Pacific Northwest: 50 Romantic Getaways
Coastal, mountain, and island hideaways in Oregon, Washington, and British Columbia

With more than 150 color photos in each book, these are the definitive travel guides to the west's most romantic destinations.

Free Travel Update
We continue to discover new romantic destinations and reevaluate our currently featured inns and hotels, and are happy to share this information with readers. For a free update on our new discoveries and recommendations (and new books in the Weekends for Two series), please send a stamped-self-addressed business-sized envelope to Bill Gleeson, Weekends for Two Update, P.O. Box 6324, Folsom, CA 95763. We always appreciate hearing about your own romantic discoveries as well!

Our Travel Journal

Getaway date:

Destination:

Our room name/number:

Memories we made:

Index

Cast Your Vote!

Northern California's Most Romantic Hotel or Inn

Complete and mail to Bill Gleeson, *Weekends for Two in Northern California*, Chronicle Books, 275 Fifth Street, San Francisco, California 94103. We'll share your favorites in future editions.

Our favorite Northern California romantic retreat is:

_____
Name of hotel/inn

_____
City/Town

What makes this place special?

_____

_____

_____

Your name/address (optional)

_____

_____